Bent Coppers

The Story of The Man Who Arrested John Lennon, George Harrison and Brian Jones

Norman Pilcher

Clink Street

London | New York

Published by Clink Street Publishing 2020

Copyright © 2020

First edition.

ISBN: 978-1-913340-43-8 - paperback
978-1-913340-44-5 - ebook

For Shirley, Joanne and Gregg
Who never failed in their support for me.

Contents

Acknowledgements

To all of those who supported me with advice and friendship during a very difficult period:

Nigel Lilley, who has been a lifetime friend and confidant and Nick Prichard who also suffered at the hands of those we relied upon. All of my fellow officers on the 'Whispering Squad'. My wife Shirley, together with George and Jill who were there on our return from Perth. The CID officers in Perth who were so supportive of my family in Perth. Members of the press who stood by me during and after the trial. To Paul Johnson and Mark Dunton at the National Archives who guided me during my research. Julian Ferrari for coming to the rescue. Natalie Jones, Mirrorpix for assisting me in locating the required images. Will Carleton, PressPhotoHistory.com, everyone at Getty Images, www.Image1st.co.uk and to my grandson Michael for chauffeuring me around and looking after me.

A Special Thanks: to Gareth Howard, Peter and Hayley at Authoright for believing in me and making this happen.

Last but not least my gratitude to Reg Pippet, Dave Cook, and FTMB LTD for their help in driving this forward.

Foreword

My name is Reg Pippet. I have always loved music for as long as I can remember. I recall listening to Radio Luxemburg when the DJ introduced The Beatles for the very first time. Then along came The Rolling Stones who just blew me away. They were my idols from that day on. To be honest, you were spoilt for choice in those days, with so many great bands and solo artists appearing on the scene. I would have loved to have been a part of it, but my big problem was I had not quite mastered the guitar so I did the next best thing: I started driving a local band around in the early 1970s.

In September 1975 I decided to travel. My first port of call was Singapore and Malaya where I stayed for three weeks visiting the places I remembered as a child before heading off to Australia and New Zealand. I returned home in June 1976. In December 1978 I flew back to New Zealand, returning April 1979.

During the late 1980's and early 1990's rumours started circulating in various books that Brian Jones 'The Founding Member' of The Rolling Stones had not just simply drowned while under the influence of alcohol and drugs as first reported. There had been a cover up into what really happened that night. A far cry from the statement given to the press courtesy of 'Mr Fix-It' Tom Keylock when they arrived at Cotchford farm. In June 1993 after meeting Tom Keylock and Frank Thorogood, my suspicions that both men were guilty in some way of Brian's sad demise were confirmed.

During that same year I met Art Wood, (founder of the 'Artwoods') and his wife Angie, and became firm friends. I was offered the job of looking after Art, which I gladly accepted, driving him to gigs and various other functions. In 2000, while still managing Art, I was also involved with Geno Washington and soul 'Legend' Eddie Floyd.

As the years went by my interest began to fade into what really happened to Brian Jones. But! all was not lost. For in 2013 a book entitled 'The Final Truth' was published giving a more in-depth and detailed step-by step account of the tragedy and the repercussions that followed. At last, the truth was finally beginning to emerge after so much speculation. This was all down to one man's extensive research. So, my sincere thanks to Paul Spendel, for renewing my faith and giving me the inspiration to continue searching, which took me down a different path.

In 2017, I was fortunate enough to meet Norman Pilcher and having met him, I was intrigued. I wanted to know what happened, and what he'd had been up against. For it paints a very different picture from what you were lead to believe in the articles written about him. Where you could have easily be sucked into a media frenzy and taken what had been written as gospel.

Meeting Norman changed everything for me,

Being asked to write the forward to this personal account of crime and corruption, is both an honour and a privilege for me.

This is a story Norman has wanted to tell for years, where 'Truth is stranger than Fiction'. This is a true account of what really happened in London's Metropolitan Police Force in the 1960's and 1970's. The drugs, the lies, the corruption and worst of all how he was set up and sent to prison for a crime he did not commit. Betrayed by those at the top, the very people who were there to protect him.

I'm proud to count Norman as my friend and I hope you too will enjoy learning from him as I have done.

— Reg Pippet

"We were known as The Whispering Squad. We would never discuss anything in the office, we'd go downstairs to the café on the corner of old Scotland Yard and we used to sit at the back in private, and we used to talk *quietly.*"
— DC Nigel Lilley

"At no time did any member of the Drugs Squad plant drugs on any suspect during raids."
— DS Norman Pilcher,
Opening Statement

Introduction

My name is Norman Pilcher. I was a policeman in the 1960s in London during a period when the Met Police was rotten to its core. Now I have reached a ripe old age, I plan to set the record straight on a few things concerning my reputation, and that of my team. I write this story not from a bitter or pained place, but one of understanding. I was naïve at the time; I am not anymore. My hope is that in straightening out rumours and hearsay that a record will then exist which is more powerful than gossip and newspaper stories, because this record is the truth and truth is the most powerful thing of all.

The backdrop to my career was the Swinging Sixties, which most people think of as an era of celebration. Beatlemania, counterculture and social revolution were how it became popularised. The sexual revolution, and questioning authority with marijuana, LSD and psychedelic music – that's what many people stood for. So, as you can imagine, being a policeman arresting pop stars for taking drugs was not going to score me any brownie points with the public during this period of change! The thing was though, I did not join the Met for popularity; I did it for other reasons and it was not to arrest famous people, I can assure you of that. Perhaps without being able to articulate it at the time, I wanted to do something sincerely useful in this world. By preventing something bad from happening, stopping someone doing something wrong or dealing with somebody when they had done wrong, I could make my contribution. What I learnt was that the majority of people were good people. And a lot of people were simply rebelling.

I appreciated the counterculture and the youth who were agitated and then rebelling against the conservatism and the conformity of the 1950s. The establishment, the Home Office, and the government were all petrified of the new age and wanted to keep with the old ways and the Victorian values but the youth had had enough of dictatorships, old systems and old thinking. I was keen to move into the new era too; this counterculture was helping to form a new culture for all of us. They were exciting times: we were moving away from a *'when I jump don't ask why, just ask how high'* to a *'so why are we doing this?'* era, and drugs were part of the revolution. But in a certain way the freedom and the liberty the young were embracing was really just a bit of a fashion. The idea was fun and perhaps well intended – reacting to much loved films like The Beatles movie, *A Hard Day's Night*. Yet if the truth be told, it was not how I observed the streets, which more resembled the movie *Alfie*. Broken lives, scandals and murders were all very real and the drug trade was not helping matters: a lot of bad gear was hitting the streets and a lot of harm was caused as a consequence.

Amidst this rebellious culture of questioning authority, it is ironic that the team I was part of – the Drugs Squad, or The Whispering Squad as we came to be known – were in fact committed to asking questions, to promoting individuality, to bonding as a group; we were bound together by an oath of honesty, and by a shared desire to kickstart this country's war on dangerous drugs, even if that meant questioning the powerful forces within the Met. And the core issue that was affecting our work? That the Met was infected by corrupt and powerful untouchable elites, hiding behind the curtain of Freemasonry. And who were the Freemasons? Who knows, but they appeared to hold little interest in cleaning up the London streets. No. That work was for me and my unit.

The central issue was that where there was drugs, there was a lot of money involved and people operating inside and outside of the law wanted in on that. People were being paid for information, regarding the when and the where. If my squad was prepping for a bust, and dealers could pay men in the Force for advance intelligence on it, then handshakes would be made. Some of the men shaking hands walked among us and they were leaking high-priced intelligence my team were working round the clock to source. The only way for us to stop that intelligence leaking was to erase the paper trail, and that meant false entries in our books. Perhaps if we knew we'd finish in prison for it, we'd have considered a different method of hiding the trail of breadcrumbs. We were breaking rules in an attempt to try and wipe off the map drugs that were damaging people's lives and were being allowed to flow on by sources within the Met. Naturally, my team and I were required to find quiet corners where we could whisper. It was a shame we had to work this way, but we were forced to because the opportunists who could benefit from the drug trade were inside the Met.

People in my team found themselves at gunpoint and I myself ended up in prison, all because of drugs and the money that was involved in its distribution. We were a team of six at Scotland Yard from 1967 to 1972 and for forty years I have wanted to tell this story. Now the right opportunity has come along, the challenge is an old one – *fact is stranger than fiction*. It's also something to do with our nature: it seems to be a kind of human thing – that some people simply cannot help but cheat, thieve and fiddle.

I first became privy to this human factor while on duty in Covent Garden. I was handed a brown paper bag by one of the porters and was told it was for me. When I opened it, I was surprised to find a small amount of cash. I was naïve and young and I took it to the station. After I made my way to the Sergeant's office, I entered to find two sergeants and an older PC sat and counting money out on the desk. I explained what happened and was told to leave the money there for them. As you can guess, they kept the money and asked me to leave the room. This was to be my introduction into how things worked internally. As corruption in the Force began to spread, good men who were working inside the Met were being penalised via the arrival of a certain Mr Robert Mark. A man who was to become a very powerful force indeed. Out in the world I was detested by the youth and inside the Met, I was fighting to maintain integrity amidst a toxic and corrupted police force who were being rooted out by Mark like a bull in a china shop. He was without concern for any good men that remained, including those in my team, who were considered collateral damage during his great reign. With the arrival of Mark and his mission to become a Lord, my time in prison was simply inevitable.

I arrested John Lennon and several other famous pop stars from this era, but many of the arrests fans claim I made were in fact myth. During this period of Beatlemania, music fans needed someone to hate and I was that person. Subsequently, many of the stories surrounding me were not true, even if people needed for them to be so. I was the Bogeyman and I have often wondered if I was the Walrus from the album *Magical Mystery Tour*. It is very likely that the line is about me, , but almost all of the other information on the internet has been made up. As you will read in these memoirs – my final police report – I had no personal vendetta against anybody or anything; I was doing a job as I was required to do it and my relationship with The Beatles was quite amicable. Leads would come in and we would be required to follow them up, it didn't matter who was on the list. Some of those leads were well known celebrities but they received no special treatment. They were normal to us.

The Home Office wanted us to go after the pop stars with rigour, but we wanted to go after the big boys so we stopped nicking the stars and we were getting in trouble for it, so we had to start investing our hours investigating the source of the drugs out of choice. As I say, we were questioning authority in perhaps the same but a different way to the youth who thought we were their enemy. As a result, we upset the Home Office no end and our senior officers too; this was when Robert Mark officially arrived and everybody knew it was going to be a bad period in the Force.

In my memoirs, I have chosen to write much of this true story as a police report, to cut through the fog and demystify the myth. Newspapers in those days did not help matters in perpetuating folklore surrounding my team and there was plenty of incentive for them to exaggerate, fabricate and sell their stories. People like to read scandalous things; but straight down-the-line report writing is considered less desirable to the readers' appetites. I happen to think this is not so, and people in fact have real interest in the truth. Especially during this period – 1960s London.

It is true, the Met was rotten. But I don't believe that men join the job to become corrupted. They'd join the job and the corruption would be brought to them and a few of them did become corrupted, seduced by money and Masonry. And you know what they say about one bad apple. The culture in all of the enforcement agencies – MI5, MI6, Customs, everybody – is 'it doesn't matter what we do, as long as we get the result.' This approach, where the end justifies the means, is not right and it breeds corruption. I have watched it break many a good man. They call it 'honourable corruption' and 'noble cause corruption' but they have made a mistake in doing so. There is nothing honourable or noble about it. It's also a dumb way to take part in the game of life if you ask me, because the truth will always come out. Sometimes it can take decades. Sometimes it can take a lifetime. But it gets there in the end. As I have said, there is nothing more powerful than truth.

During my time as an officer, Robert Mark became well known throughout the ranks and much has been written about him to date. My personal experience was that Mark had private political ambitions with a long-term mission to become Commissioner of the Met, to become knighted and to be appointed in the House of Lords. He was, upon much reflection, a budding politician.

Many politicians, both in office and in opposition, were vehemently opposed to drugs but they were ignorant about what drugs actually were and as such, had their priorities all wrong. The Home Office demanded that any public figure – especially the pop stars – should be arrested and made a high-profile case so as to influence the young not to take drugs. Of course therefore, the edict from the Home Office was for the Drugs Squad to arrest as many high profile people as possible, in order to put a stop to the drugs trade. It was doomed from the start. All the arrests did was popularise the use of drugs and increase trade; it even encouraged people to want to be arrested by us, just like their heroes were. The Home Office also instructed Customs and Excise to seize any drug shipments so that they could prove they were doing something about the drugs trade. This in turn became a new problem, causing a turf war between Customs and the Drugs Squad, each wanting their cut from the suppliers.

We were surprised always to find the press already there at our raids, and we soon realised someone in our office was leaking information. You may have read the fabricated stories on the internet about how the Drugs Squad worked hand-in-hand with the press in order to maximise the publicity surrounding celebrity raids but as far as my team was concerned, the worst thing for us, was in fact any publicity or press! The constant leaking just added to the difficulties we faced in carrying out our duties. So my team began to huddle in a corner to discuss things out of earshot and thus we became known as The Whispering Squad.

There we were, trying to do a job, and in the background ambitious men were at it – business as usual, controlling the drugs trade, moving up the ranks and climbing the Masonic Lodge ladders. As a result of their ambitions, the work of my team was interfered with, drugs continued to flow and us silly mugs had to go away to prison. My message to the youngsters joining the force today? Don't bend the rules, don't believe your own publicity and be prepared for nonsense.

Since I left the job, I have read many books about the Force, through the '70s, '80s and '90s. Corruption was unbelievably prolific and, in every job, there they were: the Freemasons and their little boys' clubs. But boys... if there is nothing to hide, *why all the secrecy?*

I have been privileged to live the life that I have but regarding my career and my own personal arrest, facts need to be written and this record needs to be set straight once and for all.

I am Detective Sergeant Norman Pilcher, the man who arrested John Lennon. We were The Whispering Squad and this is my final police report.

Chapter 1
The Norman Conquest

'This is the first day of your life son, so show 'em what you're made of.'

Looking back, now 84, I have come to realise that this was the best advice a father could give his son.

*

Dad was a carpenter and before WWII he was in the Territorial Army. He was a sergeant in the artillery so when war was declared, he was one of the first to go. He was in charge of a battery of artillery and he served in North Africa. He was away for seven years. He was a quiet man and anyone that met him respected him: he really did a lot of work for other people. He played for Margate football club and ran teams to help the community and he was president of the local working man's club in later years. He was someone I looked up to and respected because any advice he used to give was always good advice.

We were a happy family. I had one younger sister and a great mum, who was keen to see me get on in life. She worked in a munitions factory while Dad was away. When he came home she ran a boarding house in Margate. It was a good family life and I never got into trouble, 'cause if I had done I'd have got a good old thumping! But that was the way it was in those days. I went into the building trade on an apprenticeship when school finished. I didn't like it and I waited for Dad to get back one day from racing pigeons and I told him that I fancied joining the army. He said, 'If you fancy joining the army, join it because it's good,' so I joined the army.

I trained at Woking and was part of the military police and like Dad, I went to North Africa. I was in Benghazi with the Dog Company, which was a security company, and I got transferred to Tripoli where I joined a tank unit. The Americans were there and we worked very closely with them. As I was part of the military police, I was destined to be a copper and when I came back I joined the Met.

With that all behind me, of course my dad's first words of advice were important as I went off to London. Coming from Kent, the normal thing would have been to 'join the Kent' but I didn't fancy being a country copper, I wanted a bit of action in London. It was coming up to Christmas time when the letter came. I found out my application had been successful and I was over the moon. I had plans to go and work at the post office for Christmas delivery work but because I had an army background, the Met obviously chose to select me at speed. It was 1955 and I was twenty years old.

*

As I stood outside the entrance to Peel House, the Metropolitan Police training school at Westminster, waiting to go in, I was tapped on the shoulder by a young man, his name was Gwyn Davis who was from Croydon.

'Are you here for the same reason as I am?' he asked.

'If you're joining the Met, then yes.'

He was about my height and as a Welshman, he could sing of course. We were about to go through the training together, become lifelong friends and we'd one day become godfather to each other's children. We entered Peel House, which, at the time, was just off the Vauxhall Bridge Road, and it was a great big lump of a building. I checked into reception and I thought, 'Blimey', this is a bit of okay!' It was Monday 19th December, a day I would never forget.

Gwyn and I joined eighteen other hopefuls in the main hall where we circulated, meeting the others: men who I thought were mostly ex-servicemen and there was one young woman. We were all introduced to Superintendent Tommy Wall and goodness me what a tyrant! 'Cor blimey, what we got?' I said to myself. But in a way, it was good that he was so fabulously strict. It was quite a shock to us all but we presumed that he had to be like that with us youngsters. We needed to be prepped for the streets and Tommy Wall arrived to do just that. He was the senior officer in charge of the school and was certainly able to impose his presence on any given day. He was a firm guvnor as they say, outlining all that would be expected of us over the forthcoming twelve weeks. It sounded like lots of hard work and long periods of study. He also pointed out that, based on his experience, a number of people from the group would likely choose to quit and drop out before completing the twelve weeks. I couldn't help but feel quite despondent but he knew what he was talking about and three members of our group did not complete the course.

Our first lecture was given by a sergeant instructor who explained to us the procedures to be followed during the course. We were supplied with a copy each of the 'Instruction Book' which we were expected to study in depth over the duration of the course. The Sergeant gave us a briefing on the responsibility of our position whilst performing the 'onerous duties as a constable'. He carried on to explain that once we had studied and taken on board the contents of the 'IB' we would then realise that we would have to integrate our own levels of common sense and ability to control situations to carry out our duties. I was beginning to recognise the significance of my position within society and the responsibilities I was soon to be upholding.

He also said that the course could not explain certain things, such as the 'culture' of the various law enforcement agencies in the UK, and that we would have to learn about them as we went along. It was something I did not understand at the time. I was not able to get my head around what he was suggesting: *'The course could not explain certain things?'* He was talking about the corruption and providing us with a small insight into the reality of the world that was out there waiting. Blimey, none of us knew what went on at the time. We were naïve, wet nippers. We had no idea what we would face in the future but now he had broken the ice, when it did happen... it should have come as no surprise. Corruption though, always does come as a surprise when it does turn up. You never want to see it, it feels very dirty, nasty, dangerous and wrong, and as you will see, it is very real.

As the course progressed, naturally, our team became close. The period at Peel House was very enjoyable, even with the long periods of study. A few days after starting the course we were taken by bus to Lambeth and were fitted with our first uniforms, which was particularly satisfying. It was just great getting all smartened up! And from that time on, we wore our uniform all the time, for lectures and so on, and we just got used to wearing them. I felt very happy wearing it to complete the course. Some people and even readers will assess a bobby who is proud in his uniform as being very macho, as if he is somehow enjoying his authoritative position in a negative way, like he is celebrating in his power over the public. This might be the case for some bully types, depending on the individual policeman or policewoman. Some officers genuinely feel stronger in a uniform, in the same way a soldier might feel well protected in his battle armour going out on the field. Many people in their jobs enjoy uniform and police people are no different. At the time

I had no idea that so many other people my age despised the policeman in uniform. I had perhaps been rather naïve. Needless to say, as I stood there in my new kit, prepared to complete the course and hit the streets, I couldn't know that over the coming years I was to gain a reputation which would leave much to be desired. If someone told me I'd be branded a bent copper in years to come, I'd have laughed at the time!

On the 22nd March 1956 we had completed the twelve-week course and successfully passed the relevant examinations. I had an important job to do now and the responsibility of being a constable was drummed into us all the time. And it was true, a constable carries the same powers as the commissioner. It was quite frightening in many ways. It was at around this time that I had learnt a famous saying: 'Silly and idle remarks are unworthy of notice and should be ignored.' We were taught to say this to prepare us for the real world. One can imagine the remarks one receives when out on the streets; if you were out as a normal person receiving the remarks a policeman did, you'd be turning and rolling in fights all of the time, so we had it drummed into us, to keep our heads about us and to ignore the taunts.

I was informed that I, together with Gwyn, had been posted to Bow Street Police Station in E Division. We had both been allocated accommodation at McNaughton House in Holborn. I was not due to report to Bow Street until the 26th March 1956 so I enjoyed a few days back in Margate with my girlfriend Shirley before planning to return to Peel House. Dad was particularly proud that I had done it. He knew that I wouldn't have lasted in the building game.

Shirley was a dream come true. We first met at a party in Margate when we were fourteen. What can I say? She was good looking and oh dear me, all the boys were after her. We started going out together and courted for three years, mostly on the beach and walking the cliffs. That's how Margate was when you were young. Back then you literally lived on the beach. We'd go swimming, play ballgames and we had loads of friends. At around that time it was also a popular holiday destination so it was always busy. We didn't have a lot of money back in those days, so we learnt to make use of what was around us. We didn't have a television and when TV arrived, I think we were the first family on our street to have one. When the Coronation was on for Queen Elizabeth, we had a house full of people coming to see the television – which was one of the old sets with a big magnifying glass in front of it. Looking back it was hilarious. Margate was one of those towns where everybody knew everybody else and everyone was involved with everything. It was a strong and healthy place to grow up with Shirley and we had a great time with each other. She was just the person I wanted to be with going forward in life, a loyal and accountable partner; but I was still young and before thinking about proposing to marry, I needed to keep focused on the job in front of me and the next street I was destined to walk down. That street was Bow Street.

Chapter 2
Bow Street, the Cobbles,
and the Road to CID

After returning to Peel House, the class were required to assemble in the main hall where our various postings were confirmed. It meant that the fifteen of us were spread out across the Met District. Gwyn and I were delighted with our move to Bow Street and I was happy that I would be working in the West End. It was exactly what I wanted: the adventure, the excitement, the intensity of the city. We climbed on board the coach and left Peel House for the last time.

The first stop was in fact Bow Street where, after turning into Catherine Street and on to Bow Street, we were faced with our first sight of the legendary Covent Garden and it really was in full flow. It was a mass of people like I'd never seen. Thousands of locals, tourists and traders all mixing. It was hustle bustle and full of trade and action. I looked at Gwyn: 'What have we let ourselves in for? It's chaos!' I had never seen so many people and vehicles in one street. Indeed, what had I let myself in for? The army days in Africa suddenly looked a doddle compared to London's Covent Garden.

We stopped outside Bow Street Police Station and bid our friends farewell, leaving them no doubt to face their own surprises. We turned to face our post. There was a PC attending the station entrance at the time.

'Welcome to the best nick in London,' he said, grinning from ear to ear, 'you will love it here.'

We introduced ourselves to him and he, in turn, identified himself: 'PC255 Bertie Bracken,' he said and he took us in. Amazing as it may sound, we were to become family friends and now going into our later years, we are still the best of pals. I came to know him as someone who would never hesitate to put himself up front. No wonder he was manning the station entrance that day. Good old Bertie, he'd talk to anyone, and he knew who was who and what was going on, always playing funny tricks on people. We met the Station Officer who took over our introduction to Bow Street, showing us around the station and allocating us with our divisional numbers. I was given the number E332 and Gwyn was given his: E331. These very numbers tend to stick in the minds of officers forever.

After being supplied with a truncheon, whistle, a pocket book and various paperwork, we were told that these items were our 'appointments' and were to be produced on the shift parades. Things had become serious now and I was to be responsible to carry out fundamental duties in a proper and right way. It would now be up to me to make a success of things and that meant keeping my head about me and demonstrating what I was made of, just as Dad wanted it.

The Division was split into three station areas – Bow Street, Gray's Inn Road and Kings Cross. There were three shifts in operation: early 6am to 2pm; lates 2pm to 10pm and nights 10pm to 6am. These were rotated as early and late weeks for about two months and nights for one month. This was how the Bow Street patch ran. At times horrendous, but you soon got used to it.

I reported for my first early turn shift at 5.45am to parade with some others who were aware that it was my first shift and so were quick to make me feel at ease. After producing our appointments I was paired with a senior PC who would spend the week showing me around the 'patch' as it was known. In my uniform, with truncheon ready, under the guidance and support of the senior PC, we left the station and I experienced an overwhelming rush of adrenalin. I was in the perfect position and I loved it. I was ready to learn the job and begin this new experience as a London bobby.

*

The early turn was split into two sections: the first to cover the thirteen beats which was the whole patch split up over a number of beats – the area from Trafalgar Square, Charing Cross Road, up to the courts in Chancery Lane as well as the Aldwych at the bottom of Kingsway; and the second, to ensure that Covent Garden Market could function efficiently. This was the central square otherwise known as 'the Cobbles'. At the end of my first week, due to the advice given to me by the Senior PC, I was confident that I would survive and could act on my own. I was familiar by then with all of the backstreets and where the greengrocer people were all set up. The day was busy from about 5am until 11pm and it was chaos but it was an organised chaos. It was quite incredible to observe, considering the thousands of people that were there – and yet everything worked and ran so smoothly. It was great. As an officer, you really got to appreciate the atmosphere there and enjoy the stink of the city! It was just so good and there was never any trouble there, the market porters all had a job to do and everyone knew everyone. We made sure that the traffic was flowing for the trade to continue and we played our part in the most culturally rich atmosphere one could hope to know.

The second week I worked the late turn, which was mainly beat duty plus time spent on traffic control in the area of the Strand: seeing to the theatres and the pubs and the drunks all along the Embankment. Beat duty was horrendous and the traffic was chaos. People parked everywhere, so that kept things nice and busy. With traffic control, I was expected, as others were, to ensure that I returned a number of process reports which would result in motorists receiving fines for parking offences. Because of the number of theatres in the area, parking your car somewhere was difficult so naturally people would shove them anywhere, which was good for us – the culture in this area was about 'getting your figures up' and the senior officers would be happy to do so by ticketing as many cars as they could. It was all about the figures, and if you weren't bringing them in, the boss would be 'at yer', because the fact was at the time, that the work was out there and we were required to deliver it.

During my first day of early turns, I was expecting only an easy and gentle introduction to the work. But the guvnor upstairs had other ideas. Walking alone along Henrietta Street I heard a tremendous crack coming from above me as if something had broken. I looked up and observed a section of a window frame and it was falling down. As if in slow motion, I watched it slowly float to the ground. As it was doing so, a man was walking. It was really quite bizarre but the window was falling down toward this lone soul who was stepping in its direction. The chances that they would cross paths would be more than a billion to one. There was no one else around but him. The corner of the frame stuck the man who was walking and it had happened exactly as I'd imagined. I looked around to check but there was literally nobody else about at all! It hit him right on his head. He collapsed into the pavement with what turned out to be a serious and fatal injury. Had this really just happened? Further enquiries ascertained that the window had been secured and was blown off its fixtures by a single tremendous gust of wind. If a death had happened on my first early, what was the rest of my career going to include? It certainly was not a laughing matter but at the same time, it had a comical side: the man was eating a sandwich at the time and the cause of death was in fact confirmed as 'choking on a cheese and tomato sandwich'. He must have been eating it at the time and that's what he actually died of, choking to death on the sarnie before he died from the head wound! It was the first time I ever saw a death. If things had happened a slight moment later, it would have missed him. Goodness me… it was my first day out on the beat and such a bizarre event. Poor fella.

My first night shift was another eye-opener. Most of the police made their way to the Embankment where they would find a drunk to arrest, of which there were many! Then, they'd make an arrest and contact the station for transport. I was soon made aware that this was the system of incentive, whereby a court appearance the following morning would ensure that a period of four hours would be entered on the overtime card. This obviously meant that at the conclusion of a month's stint there would be a considerable build-up of overtime for which a bobby would be paid after three months. Once more, I was beginning to understand what was meant by 'the culture' of the various law enforcement agencies, how they operated and what the sergeant at Peel House was unable to articulate and teach us. 'Once you have studied and taken on board the contents of the IB you will have to integrate your own levels of common sense and ability to control situations to carry out your duties,' I remember him saying. But what if certain officers had no common sense? And what if they had no skills to control situations?

The real attraction of both early turns and nights was that you would be involved in the market activities, walking amongst the crowds of the time and working among the salt of the earth folk who were all there to trade and work. We all had a solid rapport with both the salesmen and the market porters who had a great time dealing with the 'chinless wonders': people from Chelsea or the so-called rich couples who would stagger into the market in the early hours, after a night of wining and dining, to purchase flowers and be charged the earth, the butt of the porters' wry wit who took the mickey out of them by ripping them off. They paid top price for everything they bought, but they didn't care! We just used to stand and watch, giggling to ourselves. I became close with some of the traders, like one of the porters I met there: Ron 'the Bosh' Brody, a hard nut like they all were. You'd get strong men like Ron there who were all a bit iffy with the law (but not the bad stuff) and they would play bit parts in films as strong men. They were porters and the tricks they used to pull on each other were all in good fun. Proper Londoners having a laugh. 'Blimey, guvnor,' they'd call out to me from over the cobbles. Ron the Bosh and I ended up living two doors apart on one occasion. We really would enjoy pulling stunts on each other and if you worked the night shift, you'd end up at the Kemble's Head for a nice thick steak and eggs. It was absolutely packed until five o'clock in the morning. Fantastic!

It was at around this time I worked a particular late and as was the case, we would from time to time pop into one of the theatres. Little did I know that old Bertie Bracken was at it, planning one of his practical jokes. We'd drop into the stage doors in the theatres and have a chat to the staff and a bit of a laugh. The one I used to go to was a theatre in Kingsway. At that time there was a musical on and I'd stand in the wings and watch the show and have a look at the girls, as you do! I was standing there one night in the wings and a part of the show was when they would say: 'Call the Wozzi, call the Wozzi!' which meant 'Call the policeman', and suddenly, these big hands got a-hold of me and took me out onto the stage! And sitting in the front row at the time of the musical was our superintendent. Oh my God! Of course, Bertie Bracken had arranged it all. 'It's going to be nice in the morning when I go in,' I thought to myself. When I saw him in the morning, the superintendent told me, 'I rather enjoyed that... but don't do it again, will you!' Good old Bertie, he was a good old copper.

I was posted on one early turn week to a fixed post at Bow Street and Russell Street. My task was to ensure that the junction was kept clear and the traffic was kept moving in order to facilitate the smooth working of Covent Garden market. It was a tedious period but I really got to know the personalities working there. On one particular Saturday I was engaged in the normal banter with a few porters when someone placed an envelope in my hand. It was not what I was expecting, unusual in fact and quite mysterious to a young sprout. Needless to say, I was quite surprised when I realised that it contained money. It was a small amount but it was money nonetheless, and it wasn't mine. I returned to the station at once, made my way to the Sergeant's office and, after knocking on the door, entered, only to meet with two sergeants and one of the older PCs who was at the time counting cash on the desk. In my innocence, I explained what had happened and showed them the envelope. One of the sergeants told me to leave it on the desk, which I did in haste, and I left as quickly as I could. I went to the canteen to get a cup of tea and shared the story with one of the older PCs. 'You silly sod, that was yours!' he told me. 'It's how the market says thanks for your help.' But the sergeants had taken the money and I wasn't in a position to do anything about it. It was a little introduction into how things worked behind the scenes. Although it was small and relatively harmless, this flavour of behaviour was my earliest insight into the score that seemed to divide the two kinds of man, the one who could be seduced and enjoyed the cheating game, and the other man who chose to screen himself from such pulls and make his nature stronger.

*

On the 9th June 1956 I proposed to my perfect sweetheart, Shirley, after I had been lucky enough to persuade her to take a chance on me. We had known each other since we were sixteen years old and fortunately, she took me on. So genuine, so kind, I wouldn't want to be with anyone else. The ceremony was held back home in Margate after which we came back to Hackney where we had rented a flat on Amhurst Road. We remained there for two years until we moved into a larger flat on Theatre Street, Battersea. From there, it was easy to travel to Bow Street by bus.

Now I was a working policeman, and gaining more and more experience as the weeks were passing, my eyes had become more attuned to anything that was of a 'not quite right' kind of a nature. One day, leaving the new flat in Battersea with Shirley at home, I was travelling in to work on a Number 36 bus along the Embankment. Outside New Scotland Yard, on the top deck, I happened to witness a blue car double park beside a line of other parked vehicles. The passenger jumped out of the blue car and got into one of the parked white cars. The blue car which he got out of drove off and was then followed by the parked white car that he switched into. I noted the licence plate numbers of both vehicles together with the time. I stayed on the top deck of the bus and carried on to Bow Street to start my shift. There, I asked the operator to let me know if the parked white car I noted was reported as stolen. A short time later I was told that it had in fact been reported as stolen so I contacted the Division's Q car (an unmarked CID unit), after I had identified the owner and location of the blue car that I believed was owned by the suspects who had taken the white car. We checked the address in Plumstead, South London where we saw the white stolen car in a garage together with two men, one of whom I had seen and recognised. They were both arrested and taken back to Bow Street where they were charged with theft.

For me this had been just another arrest whilst off duty but the following day an article appeared in a newspaper with the headline 'The Top Deck PC'. Someone pointed it out to me at work: 'See you got your name in the paper,' they teased me. I was quite shocked to see my name in the paper and did not like the publicity. Although I could see benefit in the public being made aware of crime, I did not see any benefit to a policeman's name and face being made popular. If the envelope of cash that the sergeants chose to keep for themselves was an introductory flavour to the corrupt nature of men in uniform, the press glamorising a small crime like this was a flavour of the way newspapers could sell copies irresponsibly. If I was going to make large arrests and make a dent in the London crime scene, perhaps my face would be made prolific throughout the press publications. I dreaded to think about such possibilities. In fact, I couldn't think of anything worse and I threw the paper into the bin.

I was lucky enough to make a number of arrests for criminal offences during my period in uniform. On one occasion, whilst walking at the Aldwych, I was called into a building and then the manager's office. There I found a man making an insurance claim. The manager indicated that his staff were not happy with the claim he was making.

'It does not matter, I can make the claim in writing, so I'll go,' the man said but I had to respond, 'You stay right where you are until I am satisfied.'

I contacted Bow Street and passed the details on to Detective Sergeant Roy Ransom. DS Ransom then made immediate plans to visit the offices, instructing me to keep him there. 'I have checked on the name he gave you and he is wanted all over,' he told me. After the DS turned up, we took the suspect to Bow Street where Ransom made further enquiries confirming that the man being detained was, in fact, the subject of a number of arrest warrants in various names. DS Ransom later told me that I would be shown as the arresting officer and that the man would be handed over to another force that were holding several warrants for his arrest. I thought that was nice – and a start for me as it was an arrest. I was obviously very pleased with the result and I learned a lot from DS Ransom. He suggested I think about joining the CID, which was in fact my private ambition, to be out of uniform and investigating serious crime. Ransom became a kind of father figure to me, guiding and advising and he was very experienced as an officer; but those in the West End always were due to the circumstances. West End coppers were experienced in almost everything you could imagine.

I remained in uniform for two and a half years, completing my probation period, after which I applied to transfer into the CID, the Criminal Investigation Department, hoping to become an aide to the CID team at Bow Street. After being recommended by DS Ransom for the position, I was called to an interview before the Divisional Detective Chief Inspector. The interview was to be held in his office at Bow Street. There at the interview, the station Detective Inspector was also present and they reviewed my record as a PC which they both agreed was one that was 'promising'. The DCI then moved over to his office window, which overlooked Bow Street and the Opera House opposite. He pointed out at a man standing outside the Opera House and he asked me a question. 'If I told you to go and arrest that man as a suspected person, would you do it?' I thought for a moment and then I replied, 'Yes I would and then I would take him before the station officer, tell him why he had been arrested and that you, the DCI, would provide the evidence to justify the arrest'. The DCI paused, exhaled, turned from the window and looked at the DI. He then smiled and said the following words: 'I think he will do.'

I left the office with an extra bounce in my step, keen to get home and tell Shirley I just got a promotion as an aide to CID, the Criminal Investigation Department.

Chapter 3
Criminal Investigation Department

I was now an aide to CID. In other words, I was on the first rung of the ladder to becoming a permanent member of the CID – I had realised early that this was the direction I wished to progress. Being a uniformed police officer was great, but it was a great beginning. CID was going to be long hours, serious work but more importantly it demanded a genuine love for the job and the work that you were contributing. It was here where I was going to build a career and make a difference to myself, my family and the community.

I had watched the way the CID carried out their enquiries. When an offence had been committed, it would be registered into the Crime Book, kept at all stations, then allocated to a particular officer who would then make enquiries to gather the facts. Progress made, if any, would be noted in the Crime Book in black ink. In any case where there had been any arrests relating to the complaint, these arrests would be the subject of a separate entry... in red ink. It was a good system, and it was transparent.

My first day as an aide was mainly spent getting to know the various officers working out of Bow Street. DS Ransom was overseeing the twenty aides who covered the whole division, working mainly in pairs. I was paired off with PC Dave Harness who was a uniform PC at Bow Street as well so he was following the same line as myself – to become an aide. He, also, was later to become a good friend, whose family and my own would holiday together down on the coast. Dave showed me the various aspects of our work, which required us to check the Crime Book at the three stations in Division to get an idea of the areas where various crimes were most prevalent. It was clear that theft from motor vehicles was a serious problem to which we directed our attention.

Another duty all CID officers had to attend to was the keeping of an official diary, which was intended to outline the duties carried out on a daily basis. These diaries were completed on a weekly basis and signed off by a Detective Inspector. An additional record was then kept in an Office Day Book where staff recorded their movements at the time in order that their whereabouts were known to supervising officers. In reality these records were always unreliable and when we did not wish to publicise – for private reasons, locations or contacts – we would enter misleading details in the records. We would enter, for example, something like: 'Entered the public house, met the informant, purchased some refreshments,' when in fact someone may well have been spending money on something else, being out and about with the informant doing something that was specific and subject to the relationship you were trying to build in your mission of investigation; but because you'd still be paying money, to get reimbursed, you would make a small claim in the diary. This was natural to the job and an art to master.

If for example, perhaps in a somewhat slightly more misbehaving way, someone had a girlfriend somewhere, he would be on duty according to the books but more likely, he would be meeting up with her for a couple of hours. He wouldn't show that in his diary, obviously, but would show something completely different. Or he might go and see a show while he was on duty. Although he was still on the ground, he wouldn't show that he was at the theatre, he'd show that he was out on the ground. This sort of thing was done all of the time, and a lot of it was in fact essential to the development of a man's work. It happened this way, has always happened this way and always will. It was not 'corrupt' per se and it might be against general orders, but the diaries were never kept correctly for all the right reasons. In a roundabout way, life wouldn't really allow for it. There were a few gamblers at Bow Street, and on occasion, a visit to the greyhounds wasn't out of the question. Sometimes it was right that I attend a certain meeting, to build relationships, understand culture more deeply; to have off-the-record conversations that were needed in investigating crime, we would show that we were working on division. It felt fine to me to behave in this way, and as long as I chose to hold on to my moral code, I had no problem living in this real way. I was later told by an experienced detective that although the culture in the department supported a casual attitude to the keeping of the diaries, if they ever wanted to get you then they would 'get you on your diaries'. In a more sinister way, if the powers-that-be ever wanted or needed to arrest an officer, they would take them down through the diaries because the diaries were never accurate. They were a chink in everyone's armour, and the squeaky clean officer was never able to remain dirt-free if he wanted to investigate crime in London. This truth is shared with the reader in an attempt not to justify but to bridge an understanding, to offer a genuine insight. London and the Met were rotten and if you needed to walk through muck, you'd need to be prepared to get your clothes dirty. It was always a risk but you had to do it.

I soon became quite comfortable working the streets where effecting arrests did not require a great deal of brainpower. Put simply, there was so much crime in the areas that dealing with an arrest became natural, normal and easy. The most prevalent crime was car theft and that was actually the one that kept the crime figures up. Bosses want crime figures down, so you'd keep observation on certain streets and you'd guarantee something would happen like a break into a car or a van. Often, we'd hide out around corners watching people work – you'd see loiterers trying car door handles and you'd nip 'em on intent. Some guys who wanted to get back into prison knew we were about and they'd often openly just drive their hands through car windows.

Together with Dave Harness, I had decided to look at the area south of the Strand. John Adam Street as usual was packed with parked cars and in no time, Dave was pointing out a chap showing particular interest in the cars. He tried the door handles of a number of them, looking around as he did so. The man then stopped beside one vehicle and again tried both nearside doors.

'That's enough; let's nick 'im before he does any damage,' Dave said.

We quickly stopped the man, told him who we were, what we had seen and that he was being arrested as being a suspected person loitering with intent to steal from motor vehicles. After being cautioned he was taken to Bow Street and charged with the offence. I had dealt with my first arrest in the CID, which resulted in a guilty plea and a short prison sentence. To be honest, although I had 'ad a few' in uniform, it was quite a big deal to make this first arrest. The time passed very quickly with long hours being worked, arresting kids in gangs coming out of Kings Cross and Holborn. We knew them all in no time – the gangs that was. They'd wander down the West End and misbehave.

With all the work, personal time was valued and I was lucky in that Shirley, my wife, was now also working long hours in an office, so the only time we saw each other was when I was on late turn but sadly, we did rarely see each other. But when we did, we'd make the most of it, and go on out and enjoy our time. This is how things were for a policeman's wife, she'd barely get to see her husband. It's why the divorce rate was so high in the CID but with Shirley's support for my career, we'd somehow make it through the years to come.

*

When taking the path into the CID the realisation that the salary never reflected the hours put into the job had to be known. There was never any question of overtime payments being made to compensate for the hours worked, you just accepted that this was part of the job.

As an indication to the Senior Officer that I was indeed suited to work within the CID, I had to maintain a good return of arrests, as did all the aides to CID. This ensured that a healthy competitive atmosphere was retained in our unit. On a number of occasions the whole unit worked together on serious enquiries. When an elderly lady was on one occasion found dead at an antiques shop in Cecil Court off the Charing Cross Road, the whole unit worked as one. The lady had been stabbed with a Japanese samurai sword. As aides we were engaged in local enquiries and were seeking information from commuters and taxi drivers. As a result of these enquiries, a driver came forward with information that he had picked up a young man in Charing Cross Road at around the time in question. The man was carrying what he, the cabbie, thought was a sword. The young man had been taken to an address in Greenwich.

It was a pure coincidence that one of our First Class Detective Sergeants had just returned from the USA where he attended a course on the photo kit system that had been developed to identify suspects. As a result of a likeness to the suspect that had been produced by the taxi driver and enquiries made by the Murder Squad, a resulting arrest was made of Edwin Bush. He was questioned by the team and subsequently charged with the murder of Elsie Batten. On his appearance at Bow Street Magistrates Court, Edwin Bush was remanded in custody for seven days. I was nominated to escort Bush to Brixton Prison; this was the only time I made use of handcuffs. During the journey to and from Brixton, Bush found himself inclined to talk a lot, mainly regarding his deep regret. I carried on escorting Bush until he had been committed for trial when the Prison Service took over that duty. At the conclusion of his trial at the Old Bailey, Bush, aged twenty-one was sentenced to death for the murder of Elsie Batten, aged fifty-nine. He was executed at Pentonville Prison in July 1961 and was the second-to-last criminal executed in London. He has gone down in history as being the first British criminal caught through use of the Identikit facial composite system.

Whilst all this had been going on, I continued working as usual, teaming up with other aides including Ron Spiers who became a close friend. Ron was someone I did a lot of jobs with and it was a relationship where we'd watch each other's backs, and rely on one another through and through. I was lucky enough to carry out a number of monthly tours in the Divisional Q car, which covered the whole Division dealing with criminal matters. The car was crewed by a detective sergeant, aide and a class one driver, all of whom were of course dressed in plain clothes.

On the 14th December 1958, whilst we were on patrol in the Kings Cross area, a call came through: a PC was down on the Seven Sisters Road on 'N' Division. As we were near the location we made our way there. The scene was chaotic but I managed to speak to a local CID officer who told me that it appeared that the PC had been stabbed while trying to break up a fight. I asked him if he knew the PC involved.

'Yes,' he told me, 'it was Ray Summers.'

My heart skipped a beat. My body froze, it would not move, but my mouth opened.

'Are you sure it was Ray? He is a school friend of mine!'

'Yes mate, I'm sorry but it looks bad,' he said to me.

Ray and I went to school in Margate together. I recalled in that moment the day I was on uniform duty in the Strand outside The Savoy doing traffic and Ray came up to me. We had a chat about what he wanted to do and he asked my advice. I told him to come to the Met as he'd find it far more enjoyable. I later found out that he did join and went up to N division, which was North London. The next thing I knew was this, and that he had died.

There was nothing we could do at the scene so we went back to our area. I advised our Detective Sergeant what I had been told regarding the incident and he agreed that I should book off duty; later he told me that Ray had died from his injuries.

As a result of enquiries made by the Murder Squad a scaffolder named

Ronald Marwood, aged twenty-five years, was eventually charged with Ray's murder. The subsequent trial at the Old Bailey found Marwood guilty of the offence for which he was sentenced to death and that sentence was carried out on the 8th May 1959 at Pentonville Prison.

It was a very unhappy period for me, knowing that Ray was gone and how it had happened. I had gone through secondary school with him and my mind kept travelling back to that day: I kept seeing him there in The Strand – 'I left the RAF Police and had enquired about joining the Civil Police. I looked at Kent and the Met. I wanted to see you to get your advice.' I felt so very guilty. Ray had also become engaged to a girl, Sheila McKenzie – this entire story was simply tragic. The loss of Ray had been too much for me to accept, but I also learned later that Sheila had also died in September 1959 aged twenty-one years. Ray was a lovely man and I think she died of a broken heart.

*

I gained a good knowledge of how the court system operated because I spent so much time there, dealing with cases in the various courts. I didn't realise it, but this period would prove quite useful in understanding how the courts could so much resemble a theatre play, as I moved into the future and toward my own case. We presented all of our cases within the Magistrates Court, outlining the evidence and informing the court of personal records of offenders. This meant that a close working relationship was required with various members of the legal profession where it was possible to come to arrangements which suited both sides and in turn save valuable court time. There were occasions when a situation arose where strong differences of opinions were apparent with defence counsels.

On one occasion Dave Harness and I were giving evidence at Inner London Sessions in a case of theft. I had appeared before the sitting magistrate on a number of occasions and knew him to be hard but fair. He sat there for years and he was really good and over the years I came to rather enjoy going into court. As long as you are straight down the middle, know what you're talking about and tell the truth, you've got no problems. If you're telling the truth, they can go at you for days to try and pull you down but you know they can't. And they know they can't. It was here in court that I learnt how powerful truth was; in fact, it is the most powerful thing, and nobody – no matter how clever, can hide from it.

As I have alluded, the court can become a bit of a circus act at times. I was part way through my evidence, being the first in, when the court adjourned for lunch. I met Dave outside the court and whilst walking to lunch we passed the defending counsel in the case. The defending counsel gave us a hard look.

'That's the defence counsel,' I said to Dave. 'I bet you that the first thing that prat asks me when we get back is what we were discussing together.'

Dave laughed and we went to lunch as planned. I returned into the witness box and sure enough the first question put to me by the counsel was:

'Tell me officer, I saw you outside this court talking to another officer. Will you please tell the court what you were discussing?'

I looked at the judge and said: 'I discussed nothing that related to this case,' presuming that would suffice but the counsel then replied:

'Officer, I want you to answer my question and tell the court exactly what you said to your fellow officer.'

I looked at the judge, who then looked at me over his glasses, and I chose to stick to my guns.

'Our discussion had nothing to do with the facts of this case, M'lord.'

The judge looked at me next.

'Learned counsel has put a question to you, and so I direct that you answer the question in the words that you used.'

'Very well. I said to PC Harness: "That's the defence counsel. I bet you that the first question the silly prat asks when I get back is – what were you and your colleague discussing outside the court earlier?"'

There was a loud cracking sound as the defence counsel snapped a pencil he was holding which was followed by muted laughter from within the gallery. The judge then spoke to the counsel:

'Well you did ask the question!'

It was one of those moments in court that I can look back on and appreciate a kind of divine comedy to life. Notwithstanding incidents like this, I soon realised that the overall quality of counsel, both prosecutors and defence, was of a very high standard.

It was around this time that I had a conversation with an eminent counsel, who mainly acted for the defence. He told me that he derived great satisfaction from the profession but was dismayed with the time he spent cross-examining police officers who he knew were, as he put it, 'lying through their teeth.' I was taken aback by the anger in his voice but realised that he was serious in his views. A regular allegation put forward by defence counsels was that verbal statements alleged to have been made, were in fact, 'verbal' – or an 'invention' of arresting officers. The description put forward by police officers was: that a 'verbal' is a *voluntary admission of guilt* made by a suspect on their arrest, which they promptly retract on seeking legal advice. Realising the gravity of his words, I chose to take note and keep what he was sharing with me in my back pocket, at this point in my career. I was still young, but I had developed some wits and knew I had a good eye on matters. There were a few things at home I needed to get organised but after that I knew I'd be able to focus on my mission to become a detective sergeant.

Shirley and I hoped to buy our own house, which we did in 1961 and we moved out of Battersea. This meant that I would have to transfer to R Division, which I did in July 1961, returning to uniform duties. It was fine. Our house was in Bexleyheath, Kent and I was posted to Sidcup Police Station, which was like chalk and cheese compared to Bow Street. The amount of crime was nominal and primarily involved housebreaking and theft. I spent two years in uniform then applied again to become an aide to CID and I was successful.

It was not an easy matter to build up an arrest record but I managed due to working long hours. I was soon appointed to the permanent rank of Detective Constable at Sidcup, working with a very experienced detective sergeant, John Callan, for three years where I was to gain a lot of very valuable knowledge indeed.

Mostly, I learned that the whole concept relied on figures and I felt that to go any further meant that it would become more 'administration' work than street work. I decided therefore to try and make it to detective sergeant. Others, of course, had different ideas and wished only to rise as far as possible within the ranks. The fact was, back then, the only method of selection was based on a healthy return of figures on clear-up rates. It was common practice throughout the service to massage the classification of complaints to reduce the true state of serious crime and this meant that offences such as housebreaking and shop breaking would be downgraded to say 'malicious damage'. Assaults would be shown as GBH Section 18 down to Section 47 or simply they'd be written off entirely. It often happened that a regular offender who had been detained for housebreaking would agree to admitting a number of cases, and show as 'taken into consideration (TIC)'.

It was common practice to run through the Crime Book with the suspect and select similar offences to which he would admit. I knew of one instance where one man admitted to housebreaking when he had been in prison at the time! All of these actions resulted in a completely false impression of the true crime rate, although it was demanded by senior officers who relied on good returns to maintain their positions and move up the greasy pole. The politicians and the Home Office would not admit to it but it certainly fitted in with their announcement of crime rates falling. This was the '60s and looking back, the numbers were being fiddled.

You see, the worth of the Home Secretary was related to the crime figures, and it was about bringing them down. That's how he was rated as successful. This filters down through the Home Office into the police service, so there was a culture where you must 'show clear-up rates'. Basically, you've got to be successful in your return of crime figures. It's all fiddling, and this was the main concern of senior officers – to get their books right, and write off crimes such as house break-ins which you can write off as 'malicious damage'. It was all nonsense. And if the truth was recorded, and the true figures released, then tourism would go down and London would go up on the list of places to avoid. This idea that 'dependence on success is equal to dependence on figures' was quite simply… nonsense! Success should be based on the honest work achieved, and with no exceptions.

Once a month the Divisional Detective Superintendent and Detective Chief Inspector would visit all of the stations, check the Crime Books and sign off our personal diaries, paying particular attention to arrest returns. If they were satisfied with an officer's return, they would sign off in blue ink. Where there had been no arrest in, say, two weeks, they would sign off in green ink; and any longer a period would be signed off in red ink and a serious warning issued to the officer to change the situation urgently. It goes without saying, nobody ever wanted to see the red.

The general day-to-day work at Sidcup proved to be very time-consuming indeed, with long hours spent at work, but living in the area did mean that more time could be given to my family. During my period at Sidcup I was lucky enough to see the arrival of our daughter, and it was certainly the most satisfying event of my life – and then in May 1966, the contentment I had with my life was doubled, with the birth of our son.

On the 27th September 1966 I was informed that I had been promoted to detective sergeant. It was a good day because at that time, I had no real ambition to reach the top of the ladder. This was the sort of rank I wanted to get, because I was still working the streets so this to me was really good and I was still relatively young, about thirty-one years old. That very same week, Gordon Taylor, a very active copper who was a very old friend of mine, contacted me to congratulate me on my promotion. Gordon had spent most of his service in the West End and asked me if I would be interested in a transfer to the Commissioner's Office at New Scotland Yard. Apparently there was a vacancy on the Drugs Squad. I said that I was interested and Gordon arranged a meeting with Detective Chief Superintendent Wally Virgo in the West End.

Bearing in mind that any contact I may have had with senior officers was minimal, I was apprehensive about the meeting. Also, I didn't know anything about the Drugs Squad. You never tended to hear of drug problems in Sidcup so I was quite naïve but I did think that Scotland Yard would be great. Just the idea of Scotland Yard was exciting enough.

Gordon and I travelled up to Soho where we met Mr Virgo in a nightclub. It was seedy in a glamorous way and immediately demonstrative of his character. He was in charge of C1 (Crime 1), and he was totally corrupt. There he was, enjoying a meal and a spread of drinks when we met. It wasn't me, at all. I knew that he was the Commander of COC1 (Commissioner's Office Crime 1) at New Scotland Yard and this department consisted of a number of specialist squads – Obscene Publications, the Antiques Squad and the Drugs Squad amongst others. C1 also operated as the reserve office to the whole of CID and was open all the time, dealing with all enquiries coming in from outside. Everything – all outside information – to do with CID, therefore, was concentrated on that one office.

Mr Virgo asked me if I was interested in a transfer to the Drugs Squad, which had a vacancy for a detective sergeant. I was interested and he told me that I would be joining the department from the following Monday. After a few drinks, Gordon and I left Wally Virgo to his meal and God knows what else. On the journey home I had to say a few words,

'I am a bit surprised to see someone of his rank enjoying all of that – what was obviously a freebee evening in a club.'

A nightclub like that was totally out of my comfort zone, but to meet a detective chief superintendent – blimey, you'd very rarely see one, let alone sit down and have a drink with one. He was wining and dining away in there – cor. Yep, I was a bit innocent and history has shown us how corrupt Virgo and his cronies were: overseeing Obscene Publications (the 'Dirty Squad') and getting up to who knows what in the porno scene.

'It's about time that you came off Division. That's the way it is up here,' Gordon told me.

My journey toward understanding how things operated and the truth of matters had just begun. Obscene behaviour was something I was about to become more familiar with, through a woman I was about to have a business relationship with – a prostitute called Eve.

Chapter 4
A Prostitute Called Eve

I'd heard about Scotland Yard. Everyone had, and so much so that we were all in awe of it. On the 3rd October 1966 I reported to New Scotland Yard at the COC1 offices in the old building on Victoria Embankment, only to be rather disappointed. You see the sign there, but then that's sort of it, so it's a massive anti-climax. When you consider it though, Scotland Yard is in fact only an administration centre. It's got a few squads that work out of Scotland Yard but people aren't taken there to be charged. So in actual fact, the nitty gritty is not done there at all. That's just where the press go, so after the usual introductions I was directed to an office above a coffee shop in Derry Gate where I met the Detective Inspector and a Detective Sergeant in the Drugs Office. I knew little or nothing about the misuse of drugs at that time as they were not prevalent outside of Central London and there seemed to be very little activity in the department with only a Detective Inspector, one Detective Sergeant and two Detective Constables in attendance. Growing up, I didn't know anything about drugs. I wasn't even much of a drinker!

I spent my first few weeks getting to know the workings of the Commissioner's Office (CO) and Crime 1 (C1) in particular. There were ten detective superintendents attached to C1, each of whom was in charge of a particular department. These superintendents were, in fact, the basis of the Murder Squad but were on call for any outside requests for assistance; Chief Superintendent Wally Virgo, who I had met that night in Soho, was one of them. There was a rotation of each superintendent, assisted by a First Class Detective Sergeant, on a 24-hour call-out system to go anywhere and take over any of the major enquiries. The superintendent in charge of the Drugs Squad at the time was Jim Barnett who was good as a leader. He was another firm but fair man – very much needed in such environments – who was supportive of his staff mostly by being totally measured. I didn't see him often because of his duties elsewhere but knowing he was in charge was encouraging considering my lack of experience. I made myself conversant with current legislation regarding the misuse of drugs and the current situation regarding the problem in London generally. As I could see it, there was a little bit of heroin here and there but people using heroin could also get their prescriptions from their doctors. There was, though, quite a bit of cannabis about. Mostly, it erupted in the late '60s/early '70s period after the pop groups became known. I spent a good deal of time together with Gordon Taylor who introduced me to his many contacts in the Soho area and these contacts were to prove invaluable to me in the months ahead with my work and investigating leads.

Although the number of staff was low there was a good atmosphere in the office, which also included four detective sergeants whose duties were to maintain checks on registers kept at chemists and pharmacies throughout Greater London. On several occasions I found myself on duty in the office alone – our detective inspector was not exactly labour intensive, spending most of his time in local public houses trying to drink them dry.

*

I quickly learned something rather unique to drug offences. This being that they were very easy to prove. To educate the reader on this point: you're there when the offence is committed – you get a search warrant, you search the property, and you find drugs. It's all over, short and sweet. Because the people are there *when* the drugs are found, by default that offence has been committed, because you have found the drugs. And the only defence they ever had to it was: 'Oh, you planted drugs on us.' This response was a natural reaction to the unique nature of how easy drug offences were to prove. The reality? Now let's be fair, were we really going to drive around in cars and plant these things in people's houses? It was nonsense. As I will share, there were enough calls coming through and search warrants to keep the entire office occupied. In no time, we had so much work coming through in fact, that we were quickly turning away as many cases as we took on, and even during the early searches, I'd flush a lot of it down the loo with the youngsters. And if the guvnors knew I did that, there'd have been hell to pay. As I was saying it was a simple offence to prove and you didn't have to go out and investigate anything. Anyway, this story with drugs busting begins elsewhere, and with an informant, a friend I was to make, a prostitute called Eve.

The office phone was always busy with calls offering information regarding persons in possession. I found it to be prudent when dealing with these calls and became quite selective about those on which I considered taking any further action. I answered one call that came through which brought information regarding an address in Bayswater. The owner, Eve, was said to be in possession of cannabis. The caller did not give their name and hung up the phone. I later checked out the address and confirmed that it was visited by men and so far, it appeared to be a legitimate call. After further investigation, it appeared to be a well-maintained property so I obtained a warrant at Bow Street to search the premises and decided to execute the warrant on a Saturday morning.

I was alone that day so I contacted a detective sergeant that I knew on Division who agreed to lend a helping hand. The door was answered by a woman and she was told the reason for our visit. We entered the flat, which was very well appointed indeed. She was a bit concerned about our entering the bedroom but we did nonetheless. We walked in, unsure what to expect, and there on the bed lay a naked man, naked apart from a sheet over his waist and his wrists were tied to the bedposts. He was angry, as one would expect and he demanded to know what we were doing, which also was to be expected. I tried to calm him down, explaining that we were executing a search warrant and I assured him that we were not interested in arresting him and that we would leave him be in no time. None of that worked in calming the naked man. He was passionately furious. I had recognised him: he was in fact a well-known Conservative MP. I decided to leave him alone to consider his position in private, and 'cool down' a little.

I searched the rest of the flat, found small quantities of drugs and told Eve that she would be arrested for possession. She was a smart girl and told me that she did not use the drugs herself, but in fact kept them to keep her clients happy. Meanwhile, my colleague could not stay any longer and he left. It was just Eve and myself and she began explaining the nature of her work and how she only dealt with upper class clients, one of whom, the man in the other room, was still shouting through the walls, roaring with all kinds of threats and pleas. She confirmed that the man in the bedroom was, as I had suspected, an established MP; apparently he was one of her regulars. After a discussion regarding her contacts, she agreed to act as an informant for me as long as it did not involve her clients. I saw how Eve could prove to be a very useful person to ally myself with. I could see how she would supply much useful information that would help reduce the amount of drugs circulating in London. There was business to discuss but with our friend in the next room screaming and shouting, we decided to go for a little walk outside, leaving her client, the disgraced MP, chained to the bed.

We went out for a coffee and we began to discuss matters. I could see that Eve was reliable and accountable. I immediately trusted her and we agreed that if she was charged for possession, it would involve her client and that was then not a good idea. I chose to dispose of the drugs I had found down a toilet and suggested Eve return to her flat after a couple of hours to inform her client that she had settled the matter and with no comeback. I told her to wait those few hours; 'Let him sweat it out,' I instructed. And she did just that.

I was not to know it but this business relationship with Eve would last for five years, during which time she'd produce good results without any problems. I did learn that her client list was widespread and involved many prominent people including, much to my disappointment, some of our own high-ranking officers. I respected the way that she ran her business, never coming into contact officially and I suppose it can be said that this was my first brush with those who governed us. It most certainly wasn't the last. I was going to learn in the coming years where and how the powers-that-be would lurk and how they would operate outside of the law, as if they were above it. The raging's of the parliamentary member chained to the bed were quite expressive of his sense of superiority. He was breaking the law, had been caught – literally – with his pants down, and yet barked at me without guilt, as if his rights were being breached. I came to observe this raging quality evident often in the higher echelons. It would remind me at times of an upset teenager who was angry at injustice.

My integration into the work I was doing was complete; I was by this time fully immersed. I had established connections, informants and I was good at the work. The searches and the investigations that followed would gradually shape and guide my future. The most important thing – I loved the work, the long hard days, and the team I was working with was establishing itself. I was still working alone quite a bit, but I could see in the future, somewhere, a solid and unified team was available for me that was accountable and reliable. It was all coming together.

*

From intelligence received, we carried out a search in Central London from which we arrested a young woman for the possession of some cannabis. She was duly charged, fingerprinted and I began noting her antecedents – which is an opportunity to learn the background of offenders. During this talk she chose to blurt out how she was the daughter of a senior cabinet minister. I knew immediately that I could expect the usual approaches for favours to be done; I was already used to the process.

On our return to CO I issued the standard notices regarding the arrest to all the senior officers around CO and the press Department, making sure that none of my team discussed the sensitive matter. The next day I had not been in the office for long when I received a call from 'a Superintendent' in 'A Department'.

Caller:	'I hear that you have arrested the daughter of a senior minister.
Reply:	'Yes, she is in court this morning.'
Caller:	'Well I would like you to be careful how you treat her. Make sure that you do not talk to the press.'
Reply:	'We do not talk to the press and she will be dealt with the same as anybody else that we deal with, Sir.'
Caller:	'Right, be sure that you do. I will be watching as I am sure the Commissioner will, Sergeant.'

At this point the call ended. I had expected calls and the boss of C1, of course, asked what had happened but never questioned our handling of the case. I later received a call from a chief superintendent who I knew well and who I respected. He wanted to pass on a message from the girl's father to me. The message was simple: that he, the father, did not want any favours in this matter and that his daughter should be dealt with in the normal manner. I respected his attitude and the girl pleaded guilty to the offence and was fined. This was just a small portrayal of how senior officers used their positions to do favours in order to push themselves upwards.

I continued to receive information from a number of informants about the activities of various well-known celebrities. Among them was the well-known composer Lionel Bart; we paid him a visit at his mews flat. We were in West London and after the usual introductions we searched the premises and recovered small amounts of cannabis. Bart was duly arrested and later charged with possession resulting in his conviction and being fined.

At about this time we also executed a warrant to search premises in West London occupied by pop singer Dusty Springfield. To say that Springfield was not happy with our visit is an understatement. As was usual in these situations, we jollied her along and ignored her foul language and her insults while we tiptoed over and all around all kinds of things. The house was messy and chaotic. She lived in absolute shit! The search resulted in restricted drugs being found and Springfield was arrested and later charged. On her appearance before the magistrates, Springfield pleaded guilty and was fined for the offences. She was a great singer, but she was using drugs and she got done for it. As a person, I don't think she was particularly nice, but there you are. Maybe she was just having a bad day, and getting done by the police for possession I would imagine would constitute pretty bad as far as days go! The expressions of the people were always the same, 'I've had better days' the faces would convey, so there was never any point in asking how they were doing.

During the following months our work rate increased with the result that our staff numbers increased. The whole of Scotland Yard was then moved to new offices in Victoria Street, which were far more suitable for us all. The squad was then staffed by Detective Chief Inspector Vic Kelaher who was now our new Chief Inspector to supervise the squad, along with two detective inspectors, seven detective sergeants and two detective constables, including Morag McGibbon, a great girl who I really enjoyed working with. She was a true Scot and someone who was straight down the middle, the epitome of the words honest and dignified. She knew the job backward – and everyone wanted to use her on cases. Sometimes they'd use her to play the 'buyer' for things like diamonds and the like. She was totally and utterly dependable and reliable and I felt safe with her but regarding the new boss Kelaher... After a bit of digging around, the facts seemed to be harder to understand. On paper he was red-hot and a very good police officer with loads of arrests but in no time I could see that he was a man who played things very close to his chest – and this was in fact an understatement. He didn't tell you a single thing he didn't want you to know, ever, and naturally I had my suspicions from early on about him. Things didn't feel safe, and I didn't know why.

The new offices were better and we also had two dog handlers on call as the use of dogs was essential to our work. The first occasion the dogs had been used was during a case in Brixton. A number of people had been arrested and charged with supplying cannabis resin. The case was heard at the Inner London Session where 'not guilty' pleas were entered. During the prosecution case evidence was given by PS Shearn, the dog handler, explaining how his dog had uncovered large quantities of the cannabis resin. The presiding judge stated how this was an early case where dogs had been used and ordered it be for the court to witness their effectiveness. Under the directions of the judge, the court was cleared and he and his clerk hid a small amount of resin within the court. The parties concerned in the case were allowed back into court. PS Shearn returned and allowed his dog to carry out a search. As I had witnessed before, the dog was encouraged to move freely among the various areas eventually making its way behind the judge's area, where, after a short time it indicated an interest in a seat next to the judge. The dog concentrated on a cushion on the seat, which in fact, had a small piece of cannabis resin pushed under a button on the cushion. The judge confirmed the find and that he was satisfied that the dogs were effective in their work.

The female defendant, who was the alleged leader in this matter, then shouted out loud: 'Jesus Christ in heaven... getting us all locked up in prison!' The trial eventually came to close with verdicts of guilty in each case. When passing sentence on those convicted, the judge addressed the woman:

'You were correct Madam', he said, 'in your remarks earlier, you are indeed going to prison for three years.'

As a result of that case the use of dogs in the area was accepted by the courts. Until this happened, people didn't really believe that dogs could do this. This trial was precedent-setting.

*

In the spring of 1968 information came to our office that a student named Kalniczky had set up a laboratory in Wapping to produce LSD together with a chemist named Malcolm Sinclair. Also involved was another man named Ken Lee and a West End club owner. As a result of observations made, both Sinclair and John Conway were arrested on the 19th June 1968 and charged with conspiring to supply LSD. It appeared to me that Sinclair was a very clever chemist and he explained to me that the chemicals in which he was dealing were not in fact restricted. He knew more about the science than our chemist did. I had long discussions with him, as a result of which my knowledge regarding the production of LSD was greatly enhanced and I soon learnt first-hand how very dangerous it was.

After their committal to the Central Criminal Court, it was decided to withdraw the case against both Sinclair and Conway. Meanwhile, Ken Lee, who had fled to Spain, returned in 1970 to be arrested subsequently in the USA. As a result of the publicity surrounding the squad a vast amount of information came to the office. I had at that time a list of twenty-plus informants who were supplying reliable information. Once more, I became very friendly with Malcolm Sinclair and while he was a brilliant chemist, I did not like what I learnt about LSD. If it goes through the skin, you're off with the funny people! On one occasion I unfortunately picked up some of the content on my fingers and experienced a bit of what they call a trip, so I do know its effects. Nowadays people wear rubber gloves and masks to guard its dangers. People take it and think they can fly around the world. It's not funny at all. The idea of it is celebrated but the dangerous consequences are seldom considered.

For these very reasons, it is not surprising that the Home Office were encouraging us to arrest the pop stars that were glamorising the use of psychedelics and with that, I began to arrest members of a rather well-known band. They were called The Beatles.

Chapter 5
John Lennon's Arrest

On the 18th October 1968 I decided to act on information I had gathered in relation to John Lennon. I had obtained a search warrant for premises at 34 Montague Square, W1 – a ground floor flat occupied by Lennon and Yoko Ono Cox. Quite frankly, we all knew they were 'at it' and we weren't allowed to provide special treatment for famous people. Furthermore, the Home Office were breathing down our necks to move on more of the big names. I did not agree with the Home Office pushing us to arrest the pop stars specifically: I needed to follow normal process and amongst my team, it did not matter what the person's name was: Ben, Simon, Phillip or John. It did not matter and it should not matter. They were a name on a list. Arresting the musicians to make an example of them and wipe out drugs was a futile attempt to handle something as permeating as drugs – that was my view. All it was going to do was add fuel to the fire.

I used to wear a postman's hat sometimes, hoping that if they'd look through the peephole, they'd not get worried. Detective Constable Nigel Gunning, tried to get in the back window but they shut the window on his fingers.

After gaining entry to the flat at around 11.55am we found Lennon and Cox on the premises. They were stark naked! The search was carried out in the presence of their lawyer resulting in a small amount of cannabis being discovered by the police dogs in a binocular case, and so it had to be dealt with. They were both duly arrested and taken to Paddington Green Police Station and charged with possession of cannabis resin. Of course the press were everywhere, which is not what we wanted. Whilst carrying out the formalities afterwards I had a discussion with John who expressed his strong views on life in general and his basic position: that his use of drugs was a matter for him and that he was the only one who could decide on how he treated his body. This was a view that I had heard many times previously. There was no aggravation at all and his ideas of peace and kindness were expressed in his demeanour and attitude, which was quite humbling indeed.

Of course the allegations had begun that we planted stuff on him. On the 28th November 1968 Lennon and Cox appeared at Marylebone Magistrates Court where John was fined for possession after pleading guilty. I later received a case of brandy for the troops in the office from John Lennon's lawyers together with signed copies of his record albums. I was a very lucky man indeed.

During the course of this case I came to respect the views expressed by John and it was as if he had taught me a thing or two. In the future when he was touring, he used to send me postcards from Japan: 'You can't get me now,' he'd say, joking around. No one can deny that it was a perfectly amicable relationship.

As a result of this search a question was asked in Parliament by an MP who questioned our actions and suggested that perhaps I should have informed John Lennon of our intended actions. What a ridiculous question to be asked in Parliament! If John Lennon had been warned, he'd have flushed the gear!

John Lennon taught me that his use of drugs was a matter for him and as he said, he was the only one who could decide on how he treated his body. This position is quite fair and I have had much time over the years to reflect on his way. As I have already stated, this was a view that I had heard many times previously. People would always talk about how I could go out and get as drunk as a parrot so why couldn't they do as they pleased? It is a fair point and a good question to ask. People used to also say, like Prohibition in the States: all it does is increase the crime rate, which is also correct.

The larger questions surrounding the drugs issue were beginning to surface and going after famous people to make an example of them on behest of the Home Office was, as I have said, a flimsy means of attempting to get drugs off the streets. This 'trying to make an example of' method was in fact prolonging and celebrating the use of drugs, now that the youth wanted to emulate the rebellious nature of their heroes.

Back then, I began to warn my seniors that cocaine would be the most popular drug and today it has become so. Cocaine is everywhere and especially amongst the middle class bankers who work very stressful jobs and need to relax. You become addicted very easily and the drug anaesthetises the reality of the stress, which people don't want to face or deal with, as it may require changing life circumstances. You can't stop it because there is not enough manpower to do so, and you can't put everyone in prison. Trying to deal with the drugs issue only in law enforcement is an absolute joke, as I realised from early on in my career. I didn't want to have to arrest John Lennon and doing so was farcical; he was well aware of that.

Although the Home Office were naïve, they were well intentioned. Often our decisions to use drugs are influenced unconsciously through the culture and without our own knowing. Cigarettes are culturally very engrained and they don't do us any good. Advertising sold the product and made smoking fashionable in this way, so there is a fine line between what a person chooses and how they are influenced. The industry sold cigarettes by advertising them as liberating and fashionable, mostly through print ads and the movies. As a result, cigarettes cause thousands of deaths each day and on average, smokers die ten years earlier than non-smokers. Smoking causes cancer, heart disease, stroke and numerous lung diseases but because the tobacco industry spends money every year on advertising we tend not to care; 'I could get hit by a bus tomorrow' is often the way it's looked at but this is a rationalisation so we can keep smoking, drugging and drinking. It is a vicious cycle.

Upon reflection, I feel obliged to share my thoughts regarding the use of alcohol, cigarettes and drugs to escape life's hardships – this is exactly why we take pleasure in them. I look back on the work we did at the Squad and like to think that we were somehow making things a touch more right; that's what we wanted to achieve. But to really make a difference, we should legalise drugs and bring them above ground. This is what we must do, of course, due to the illegal activity and the corruption it creates but people still don't see the sense in legalising drugs. Eventually, they did see the sense in legalising alcohol again in America. Drugs, cigarettes but especially alcohol help a person care less about the responsibilities he or she faces but this is because it dampens anxieties; it is a very dangerous aid and it allows people to do 'stupid' and 'fun' things and celebrate all of the time.

This was the new vibe in the 1960's, that life was one big party, but out there with my face up close to the consequences of the big party, I saw it differently, and I saw the damage up close and personal. For this reason, I was not a big drinker. The culture of the time was 'freedom, freedom and more freedom' but there was something not quite right with celebrating in all of this unlimited freedom. There was something irresponsible about it, and although I did not wish to judge it, I did see the dangers in it. I never assumed an 'I know better' position with regards to drugs and alcohol but something was not right during this era. There was an imbalance. My own pleasures?

It was more to do with the deep satisfaction I was experiencing through my work: it felt meaningful, and it was as if there was a secret satisfaction I was able to experience – one that I wanted others to have. I found that you could get more pleasure from life than the young were all falling into with the sex, drugs, alcohol and unrestrained levels of freedom because what I had experienced was beyond pleasure, it was purpose. I saw the despair and the pain and the suffering that the pleasure seeking was creating, like with my friend Tubby Hayes, and I wanted to do my bit to stop people experiencing the downside.

John was right about what he told me, regarding himself, and it was an honour to have such a dialogue with him; but if I meet him beyond the pearly gates, I would like to talk with him more on the matter! For example, if a youngster who admired Lennon chose to model him, this youngster might also feel inclined to make use of such drugs. This was the Home Office's argument. Having had children, I know that it is often the case that they are not the most responsible judge of how best to self-medicate. A drug addict is very often not the best judge of their own best interests: friends, family and a strong community often can be. Marijuana when smoked tends to increase the chances of a person experimenting further and often such experimentation takes place in dangerous environments that are attractive and tempting for the adolescents modelling their heroes, who encourage the use of drugs through their music. I believe such states of increased or alternative awareness and even peace itself can be achieved in a more satisfying and worthy way than using drugs.

I liked John very much and his peaceful intentions but I do not believe that drugs are in anyway the bridge to peace. Far beyond it in fact. I am sure John did not believe so either, but I think a bit of him did. I have seen many sad things happen to drug addicts that can break a man's heart. A man is free to do as he chooses but these choices are sometimes not completely wise. I do not claim to know all that is right but I do not believe that drugs should be illegal even though for most people, using them is not a good idea; but I appreciate there are many sides to the discussion. The backdrop to my working days was a counterculture that was rebelling and experimenting but because of what I saw drugs do to people, it was difficult for me to accept them as good for the human soul.

We needed to influence the Home Office. If we were allowed to somehow go after the dealers, it might make a difference, we began to think. We did about eight celebrities in the end out of dozens that we arrested for possession but at the end of the day, a few ounces of cannabis in someone's pocket was not what we were here for or after and that's when we stopped. I didn't like the allegations made against us in the papers – because they were untrue, about how we were planting drugs in people's homes and then arresting them for it. I wanted to change things, not just make easy arrests. I just wish John had told me that it was Jimi Hendrix's weed in the house because I'd have had a job to prove it wasn't – but he chose to plead guilty. Of course, the press hyped everything up which none of us wanted. We really didn't want it, with pictures all over the place of us. How could we do the job now there were pictures of our faces? People now knew who we were and fame is the last thing you want if you're working under cover. Considering how small a part arresting pop stars was to us, the episode was very much an example of how the press would make a mountain out of a molehill to stir the appetite of a reader, and create a bogeyman for the youth to hate.

I was later to learn much regarding the story of drugs, the use of them and our world's addictions to them. Joe Bolton, who became a new Inspector, came out of Bramshill and Joe was the first person who sat down with us all and began to talk and teach us about the history of drugs and addiction. He had written a dissertation on it all, he was reliable, knowledgeable and able to educate us on things we needed to know about. He was also able to testify how straight we were as a unit, and because he could see that in us, he wanted to invest time in us and teach us a thing or two. He was the first one who began talking about how this goes way back, to the Bible and the Hashemites and that that's where it starts, and he ran the entire timeline forward for us. The frightening statistic came after the American Civil War. The only thing they had to kill pain was morphine and this produced something like 850,000 morphine addicts. The mind tends to drift back to the Wild West, where there are all these soldiers addicted to morphine for pain. So this problem existed in America since those days, and because nobody thought to legalise it, it became the industry that is as big as the entire economy of America. He educated us and we got hold of the MIMS chart of drugs in the UK, and in no time knew every single tablet and what it was and what it was for due to Joe's work and deep study into the history of drugs and what they are chemically. We began to carry these charts round with us because these were the days before the internet and Wikipedia where today a person is able to build their general knowledge at speed. There was little time to disappear into the library archives also, and we needed to educate ourselves professionally and not via the media and the pop stars who were illustrating their hallucinogenic experiences artistically. Such attempts to outline what drugs were and what they did were carefree and idealistic. Nobody provided us professional and mature information except for Joe and he was the only one.

After sitting with Joe, I began to get my head around even more regarding this business, and why drug offences did not file as recorded statistics. They were non-reportable crimes, so it didn't help the figures anywhere and so there was little incentive to run programmes to teach officers what drugs are, where they came from, what they do and their potential dangers. Consequently, drugs as a trade spread like wild fire. The only thing arrests did was generate more publicity which was adding fuel to the wild fire. To understand this story objectively, we needed as a team, to stand back from the canvas and understand some serious fundamentals:

1. Drugs were soothing man's suffering whilst moving him further into negative dependant conditions.
2. Trade was widespread throughout the world.
3. In the UK, offences were not recorded statistics, and all the Home Office wanted were stats because stats were measurable and measurements allowed for men with career ambitions to climb higher and progress in their status.
4. Due to the above, any attempt to correct or slow the virus was tantamount to moving an immovable object.

As the reader may finally be able to grasp, the Home Office encouraging us to arrest pop stars in an attempt to 'put a stop to the drugs issue' was beyond laughable, it was in fact infantile. Add to this, the harsh reality that powerful men within the Yard like the commander of C11 – the intelligence department – had all the secrets within the Met and was colluding with the biggest villains was making a bad situation a lot worse. There was even talk that two guys on the Flying Squad were working for the team that we were about to nick. The Met was rotten to the core, and we were out arresting John Lennon – a singer songwriter who was generating British culture. Like I said – it was infantile.

Correct measures to implement programmes that take into account the width and the breadth of the drugs issue stand a chance only through legalising natural and chemical compounds. In any other circumstance, people will always locate something herbal and natural, or manmade to placate his or her suffering in life. The idea that marijuana was natural and so must be respected and used as a medicine was not an opinion I tended to agree with; did you know that Socrates was put to death after being forced to drink poisoned herbal tea?

Addiction in a positive light can mean devotion, in the same way a person can be devoted to their work, their morals or their partner and family but when they become addicted negatively, they are in need and they are in dependency and this is not a healthy relationship to have with medicines that can damage and weaken. An addictive substance that causes a temporary high or which eases pain a little and then provides a deeper low will tend to create an addictive habit as the person is then caught in the repetitive pattern. This pattern can send a person spiralling down, instead of building them strong. When the addictive substance then offers the hope of saving a person from their pain, they are drawn to it and it is a very hard and serious problem to solve, especially when the conversation and the substances are all kept hush-hush and underground. I believe John Lennon had a strong insight into all of this. He made it to America but he's gone now, though his spirit lives on, and it will do forever.

Chapter 6
The Death of Brian Jones

As a result of the increase in staff within the Squad it divided into two units, one organised by DS Phillips and the other by myself, DS Norman Pilcher. I was fortunate that those joining me were Detective Constable Morag McGibbon, and Detective Constable Nigel Lilley, a very fine gentleman indeed.

Nigel was a different kettle of fish from any other officer I knew. He was a public schoolboy who came from a military family. He'd been in the job for five years already and he worked in Chelsea a lot so he had good experience regarding what was going on across the field. I remember when he first arrived and when I first met him – I was a bit taken aback, mostly by his style of dress, which was to say, absolutely immaculate. When he came walking down the corridor that day, I remember the Superintendent walking past leaving some remark about 'male models' to try and bring him down a peg, but he was experienced and ahead of all the games being played – he was completely trustworthy, reliable and in my view, above the rank he was given. He was good, he knew what he was doing and how to deal with people. When Nigel transferred over to the Drugs Squad I was quick enough to grab him one afternoon.

'How come you got the transfer?' I asked him and Nigel told me the entire story.

'I told my boss that after a week working in Obscene Publications, I didn't want to see another picture of anybody screwing anybody else again. So they did me the favour.'

'Really, is that how it happened?'

'Pretty much, Nobby. The guvnor didn't like me being there, and he wanted to move me down the corridor into fraud and the misuse of public funds. I went there and it was good, but I heard about "Nobby's Team" and here I am.'

Nigel wanted to join the team, so we were quid's in there and he was to be my right-hand man, a real boon to the forming of the Squad. Also joining me was Nick Prichard, Nigel Gunning and later, Detective Constable Adam Acworth. Both Nigel Lilley and Nick Prichard were very experienced in the CID and Morag McGibbon was an exceptional asset to our unit while Nick was keen to act in an undercover role to which he was well suited. We were The Whispering Squad, and my team was united. It was exactly what I wanted going ahead.

The Squad was supervised by Detective Chief Inspector Vic Kelaher who had moved to us from C8, the Flying Squad. As mentioned previously, I knew of his reputation as a well-informed investigator who was basically, a lone wolf keeping everything close to his chest. His father had been a detective sergeant who died very young, leaving Vic to spend a period in the police orphanage; after joining the service, he soon made his way through the ranks and became – the guvnor.

*

We'd always get sent through a lot of intelligence on Brian Jones, the founder of the Rolling Stones – he mainly dealt with prescription drugs but he did like the other stuff too, on occasion. He gradually began to move up the list of those to be looked at and my intention was to get a warrant to search the premises. Previously, we had arrested Brian, along with his friend, the European aristocrat, Prince Stanislas Klossowski De Rola Baron De Watteville, known as Stash, and after this straightforward search, they were both charged. This earlier charge, although important to them, was not important to us at all in regards to our greater fight against the misuse of drugs. Jones however, did of course remain on our radar and so the intention to get a warrant and see to him again, had reappeared. Due to the nonsense permeating through the press regarding our relationship with Jones, I was not looking forward to a re-arrest. Previously, we had been accused of all kinds of queer things but unbeknownst to the newspapers, it often transpired that we would end up in a friendly relationship with the people we arrested. My intention to investigate matters concerning Brian Jones again, however, ended abruptly. The news I had suddenly received was very sad, but worse than sad: a chain of events had just begun which was to cause confusion, bewilderment and secrecy of a dark nature throughout the force, and indeed the country, which would last for the next fifty years.

On the 3rd July, I was told that Brian Jones had been found dead in his swimming pool. This was sad news to us but it was not surprising either, taking into consideration the life he led. My interest in Jones regarding drugs was over, but on a personal view I was intrigued in the circumstances surrounding his death, mainly because things didn't add up. The inquest into the death of Brian Jones recorded a verdict of Accidental Death after a police investigation. My own view was that Jones had met a violent death and was in fact murdered. I was convinced that Jones had been killed by his building contractor, Frank Thorogood, to whom he owed considerable sums of money for work carried out by Thorogood. My view of this matter was further supported by an allegation that Thorogood admitted to Tom Keylock, at the time of his death, that he had killed Brian Jones. Time has passed and since then, I am convinced this was a major cover up. Brian was in fact, a very capable swimmer. This whole story was a very sorry saga, which I feel, could have been avoided had we acted sooner in taking action against Jones regarding possession.

As unpleasant as he was as a man, and as hated as he was by some, he was very talented and he did not deserve death. It was totally wrong and it should have been dealt with properly as a case, but it wasn't. There was no serious enquiry made.

In the book *The Final Truth:* it is written that the Drugs Squad were involved in the cover-up of Brian's death. This was completely untrue and in the near future I was to receive an e-mail from Paul Spendel, one of the authors, who wrote to me saying:

> I would sincerely like to apologise if I ever hinted at the fact that the London Drugs Squad had anything to do with the cover-up regarding Brian Jones. This was not the case at all. It was Frank Keylock and Wally Virgo, teaming up. Nothing to do with you guys. Enjoy your break. Paul.

This was complete contradiction to what he put in the book. For the first time, he was suggesting to me that Wally Virgo was involved but why on earth would Commander Wally Virgo be involved in the cover-up of the death of Brian Jones? This enquiry was a case from Sussex; Virgo was a London policeman.

In my old age, I have tried to work out why. I think I have worked out why now, as a result of information I have received over the years gradually. I have never understood why the Yard was involved; I now understand why the Yard *could* have been involved. Wally Virgo… I used to talk to him quite a bit and he'd usually be asking us how we were getting on. He stopped me one day, asking me about Jones but nothing had been verified at this time.

'Why the interest?' I asked him.

'No reason,' he told me.

Why is he asking me about Brian Jones? I thought. This was subsequent to Brian Jones' death. The whole thing stunk and it was arranged as a straightforward coroner's enquiry into the death of Brian Jones. And herein lies the issue: it wasn't a coroner's enquiry. It should have been a suspicious death enquiry, properly dealt with by the local CID and it never happened. It's quite obvious to me that Brian Jones was murdered on the night of the party and all of the evidence points to that. It should have been properly investigated at the time but it wasn't for some reason. Maybe one day, we will find out why. It's been a real mystery for fifty years now and everybody at that party should have been seen and spoken to, and they weren't. None of this was my responsibility to investigate at the time, and so I kept my head down but eyes peeled, as I continued on with the work.

In September 1969, information came to us that a number of dealers were planning to produce LSD in large quantities. Together with Vic Kelaher we assessed the information, which was regarded as reliable. Vic arranged for the suspects' phone calls to be monitored and we started lengthy observations on the suspects who were also dealing in cannabis resin from premises in Hampstead. As a result of our observations, we identified premises in St Leonards Avenue, Hythe, in Kent, which were being used as the base where the LSD was being produced. I contacted Detective Sergeant Brian Darnell who was dealing with drug offences in South East Kent and I made him aware of our ongoing enquiries. He agreed to join our team. As a result of the telephone intercepts it was confirmed that the production of LSD was well advanced, together with the fact that the suspects had treated the upper floors of the house with inflammable paint in order to destroy evidence should they be raided. Vic and I agreed that we take action as soon as possible and together with the assistance of Kent Police we laid out the action to be taken. I decided to take precautions to cover the access areas to the premises. Our intention was to gain entry not only on the ground floor, but also through the first floor windows by using ladders. The local fire brigade put a fire tender and crew on standby in case there was a fire and I supervised this operation while other members of the Squad dealt with the property in Hampstead, where they recovered large quantities of resin resulting in the arrest of two men.

The search in St Leonards Avenue, Hythe, was successful in that minimal damage was caused, the LSD in the course of production was seized and three men were arrested. All the suspects were taken to London and charged with a variety of offences. The conclusion to this matter came at the Old Bailey when long prison terms were given to those concerned. I meanwhile had been in contact with the families, one of whom was experiencing serious difficulties but I managed to ensure that this family had a reasonable Christmas by supplying them with food to cover the holiday period.

It was early July 1970 when information came to the squad that a man by the name of Francis Morland was involved in heavy-duty cannabis smuggling into London. Morland lived in Castelnau, Barnes, with his wife. As a result of our enquiries we as a team were satisfied that he was in fact dealing in various types of restricted drugs. I discussed the matter with Vic Kelaher who agreed that we should monitor Morland's activities.

I brought the team up to scratch and laid out plans for observations to be kept on Morland to ascertain who his associates were. In August, Morland travelled to Morocco where he was introduced to Robert Palacios, an American, who had sailed to Morocco in his catamaran the *Letitia*. Morland, who was in touch with the Third Secretary at the Liberian Embassy in Rome and other diplomats, had large amounts of cannabis resin stored in the mountains in the country. Morland persuaded Palacios to join him in smuggling 200 kilos of resin into the UK using his boat, the drugs duly being loaded onto the *Letitia* and the pair made their way back to London. Further information that I received indicated that Morland offered Palacios a chance to transport a ton of resin to the Bahamas in his boat but Palacios refused and asked that the drugs currently on the *Letitia* be removed… quickly.

On Monday 5th October 1970 we kept observation on Palacios and Morland, who were taking lunch at the Cumberland Hotel, Great Cumberland Place. It was believed that money changed hands at this meeting so we continued watching both of them until Wednesday 14th October when they again had lunch at the Cumberland. I had decided that we had reached a level of knowledge to confirm that there was a real likelihood the drugs were going to be moved but we did not know at this stage where the *Letitia* was moored. It was therefore imperative that Palacios should be closely monitored.

We planned to let Nick and Adam of the team concentrate on Palacios with the backing of Morag and two other Detective Constables. Palacios and Morland were joined for lunch by a young woman and at the conclusion of their lunch the three left the Cumberland, with Morland leaving the couple to make his own way. I decided to let Morland leave without our company, instructing Nick and his team to concentrate only on Palacios.

Palacios and his companion were followed across the West End for some time before entering an American Express branch off Haymarket. After leaving that bank the couple moved down The Mall and hailed a black cab, which eventually dropped them in Holbein Place between Sloane Square and Pimlico Place. Palacios entered the car sales area of Frank Dale & Stepsons who dealt in top range cars. Nick and Adam were surprised by this move, and Adam was suggesting that he was going to buy a Bentley. In fact Palacios later appeared driving a maroon Rolls Royce with license number VBK2. He drove to Nevern Square where the woman left the vehicle and I later received a phone call in the office from Nick updating all on the situation. Palacios had passed through West London and joined the A4 heading West so I told Nick to continue following him and to not worry about leaving our borders as I would deal with that problem.

Palacios drove on followed by Adam until he reached the Isle of Wight ferry terminal and purchased a return ticket. He was heard enquiring about the return times the following day and after disembarking from the ferry, Palacios drove to Ryde and then Newport where he vanished. Nick and Adam called into Newport Police Station where they enlisted the help of the locals there to locate the Rolls Royce. The car was found at around 10.30pm in the Groves and Gutteridge boatyard parked on the quay.

At 4.45am lights were seen on a boat moored away from the quay. It was in fact the *Letitia* and Palacios was seen to be on board. He loaded several boxes into a dinghy and brought them ashore placing them in the boot of the Rolls Royce and then made three trips loading boxes into the car. At 7am he left the yard driving to the ferry, which he boarded.

I received a phone call from Nick outlining the movements of Palacios and so instructed Nick to stay on the island, to inform the local force and contact the Customs Department in order to search the boat and obtain further evidence. After we had detained Palacios in London it was imperative that any evidence left on the boat should be retained by the enquiry team as a part of the case. With the assistance of a local customs officer the *Letitia* was searched by Nick and Adam who took possession of twenty-one weights (blocks) of resin and the boat's logbook which showed details of the journey from Morocco. I instructed Nick to return to London with the evidence.

'Nobby that was good work,' Nick said to me.

'Better than nicking pop stars?' I asked him.

'Yeah,' he told me, 'this is a better gig.'

The Custom Officer's view was that they should retain the property (it was obvious that Customs were not happy with our looking into the case). Due to the nature of these situations we often crossed swords over these matters and I could not understand why there was so much animosity between our departments as we were all seeking to achieve the same results. I had no intention of backing down so I contacted Chief Superintendent Jim Barnett, our boss, and brought him up to scratch. He contacted the Customs Department involved and made it clear that we were taking possession of the evidence for production in court.

Palacios was detained after stopping at a phone box in West London. When he was approached, he threw the car keys away in an attempt to deny any knowledge of ownership of the vehicle. The Rolls Royce was searched by myself and I found the boxes of resin in the boot together with more on the rear seat. After being arrested we took Palacios and the car to Morland's address in Castelnau. Morland and his wife were then arrested together with two other men found there. Later, at Cannon Row Police Station, I drew up charges of conspiracy to import cannabis and possession of cannabis, which were put to those arrested. It was clear that Palacios was unaware that he had been followed over such a long period by our officers and the following day they all appeared at Bow Street Magistrates Court. Considering the situation, I asked that they be remanded in custody because of a flight risk and the serious nature of the charges which the court agreed, remanding the four men in custody and granting Mrs Morland bail in the sum of £1500. Nick was right. It was a much better gig.

*

In April 1970 an informant named Kevin Healy was introduced to me by Oxford CID after being arrested in possession of cannabis. Healy was in fact a heroin-dependant. On the 25th April 1970, Healy met Nick Prichard, our undercover officer, in Central London when Healy set up the purchase of LSD tablets from a man named Lewis.

I had previously met Healy who I found to be a very dangerous person indeed and I had a personal policy of not using drug dependants as a source of information. It was decided that Nick would monitor any information sourced from Healy, and he was also well aware to tread carefully when dealing with him.

As a result of Healy's information we arrested Lewis in South Kensington together with Healy who was later released. Lewis had offered for sale just over 13,000 LSD tablets for which he was charged and he later pleaded guilty at the Inner London Session to possession and was placed on probation for three years.

I later paid Healy £40 in cash and decided that Nick should finish his contacts with him; his dependency on heroin, in my view, made him unreliable and would eventually cause our department problems. Nick completely agreed with my views. My reticence regarding Healy was well founded because shortly afterwards I was informed by my contact in the Home Office that he had complained to his contacts in the CID in Oxford that he had not been treated well by both myself and Nick. This would have been true in view of the fact that we had severed ties with him. Healy claimed that I had given him 162 LSD tablets as payment for his information, which was completely untrue. The truth was that, when the LSD was seized from Lewis it was bagged, sealed and forwarded to the lab; and at no time did anyone involved in the arrest handle loose LSD. As far as I was concerned, that was a complete 'No No' – mostly in view of the fact that I still considered LSD to be the most dangerous drug out there.

I later learned, from my contact at the Home Office, that the Chief Constable of Oxfordshire had submitted a report to the Home Office outlining Healy's story. I had discussions with our team and then made it clear that if the Home Office accepted Healy's complaint, then the Home Office knew where to find me and no doubt would make their own enquiries. At no time was I informed of the allegations. By this time, I had become sick and tired of the information that I was having passed to me by the Home Office, that we were involved in recycling drugs back onto the streets. It turned out that they were at the time compiling their own file of complaints against our unit, which varied from the alleged planting of drugs to assault and thefts of cash. If the Home Office were in fact considering that such complaints were genuine, the matter should have been passed on for an investigation to be conducted. As was usually the case, weak-kneed civil servants were failing to carry out their duties and faced both directions at the same time. The actions of other units in the service were not a concern of my own; mine being the well-being of our unit who I knew always acted within the rules. We held a meeting, myself and the unit: Nigel, Morag, Nick and Adam. We sat in the same corner that we always did, at the back of the Italian café and had a bit of a whisper together. It was thought that I should go to Wally Virgo with this matter.

As a result of gathering enough information regarding the attitude and culture within the Home Office, I did then speak directly to Virgo, asking if he had received any complaints relating to our unit.

'I have had nothing from the Home Office about your work but in view of the results that you are having I should think that you have upset a few people,' he said to me.

'I have been told that there is a file being kept alleging serious matters: the recycling of drugs and even assault. Can you have a look at what is going on?' I asked him.

'I certainly will because I'd have thought that they'd have passed such serious complaints to me,' he said.

'I hope that you can sort it out – I'm fed up with my team working round the clock and being the subject of such rubbish,' I told him and then left it, utterly dissatisfied with the situation. I was even considering walking into the Home Office and demanding that if they had such allegations against us, that they pass the relevant information on to the appropriate department in order that it be properly investigated.

In 1970 I submitted a report to the Home Office outlining my views on the system of enforcement. I was later told by my contact that the report had been binned.

I had by the late 1970s come to the conclusion that the long periods that our unit were devoting to chasing around dealing with all forms of minor possession offences should not be our remit. Although we were showing a high return of arrests, we were not showing good results regarding the seizure of drugs. A few whispering discussions began within the team and we were all in agreement – that we should think about making moves on the supply chain itself. This was to later cause a good deal of friction with senior officers but the die had been cast.

Chapter 7
The Whispering Squad

By the end of the 1960s, our position at the Drugs Squad was becoming almost untenable. On the one hand, we had constant pressure from the Home Office, from our superiors and from more shadowy figures in power to keep up the high profile celebrity arrests. On the other hand, the more we as a team realised the true impact of drugs on the people of our city, the more we understood that such efforts were mere window-dressing: we needed to step forward and get to the supply.

But it wasn't just this conundrum that faced us; we were also hampered every day of our working lives by unauthorised leaks of critical information out to the press and to the criminal fraternity. Someone or some people in our organisation could not be trusted to maintain the confidentiality on which our work depended.

That's why we – a small team of just six people in the Drugs Squad – resorted to secrecy. We would now meet daily in the corner of the café and quietly share operational details to one another. Of course, it wasn't long before we became known as The Whispering Squad. But we had no choice; it was either whisper or be betrayed.

*

At about this time I was lucky enough to meet and eventually befriend a man who was a giant in the journalistic world. His name was Robert "Bob" Musel who at that stage was the European editor for News International who were based in the USA.

As a result of information obtained by Vic Kelaher, our unit made the arrest of an American national who had carried through Heathrow airport a total of 3000 LSD tablets to sell in London. We arrested him in Earl's Court in possession of the drugs and he was charged. He appeared at the Magistrates Court and was committed to trial at the Inner London Sessions.

Being remanded in custody, this situation prompted Bob Musel to contact me at New Scotland Yard to arrange a meeting to discuss the case. I met him and he told me how the man was in fact the son of a senior executive at News International. A suggestion was put forth that I approach the prosecution legal team to make them aware that a plea of guilty was to be lodged and if a noncustodial sentence was imposed the suspect would leave the UK the same day. My own view was that a large quantity of a dangerous substance had been taken off the streets and that valuable court time could be saved. The prosecution agreed to the request as a result of which a large fine was imposed by the court and the person involved did in fact leave the same day, returning to the USA where he was interviewed by the American authorities.

I came to know Bob Musel well and regarded him with great respect. Although Bob never discussed the personalities he met in his work, there were numerous stories he told regarding his work over nearly sixty years as a journalist. We had many discussions over lunch at Les Ambassadors regarding his days during the Prohibition years in the US and he considered the crime situation in those years as being totally out of control, predicting that we were heading in the same direction in the UK. He made it clear that those who governed us from behind the scenes never appeared to learn from history, but endeavoured to maintain an arrogant superior position that they knew what was 'best for all'. Bob often quoted the view that whatever politicians became involved in was certain to go 'belly up' and end in failure due to their own arrogance. I had seen this arrogance up close, it was superior in its quality: a negative version of confidence. The aphorism that, 'Power tends to corrupt, and absolute power corrupts absolutely. Great men are almost always bad men…' was his position and I was starting to understand. He was indeed a worldly wise man with many interests including his success as a lyrics writer, writing hit songs such as 'Band of Gold' and 'Poppa Piccolino'. Bob passed away on the 8th September 1999 aged ninety-one.

*

Meanwhile, the need for arrests on possession continued. It was impossible – and would have been against regulations – to ignore the mass of evidence continually presented to us. So, on we went, and on the 12th March 1969 at Claremont Park, Esher, we executed a search warrant at premises occupied by George Harrison and Patti Boyd.

On our arrival we found that Patti Boyd was alone in the house as George Harrison was absent attending the wedding of Paul McCartney and Linda Eastman. Boyd asked if she could contact George to inform him, which she did. I agreed that we would await the return of Harrison before searching the premises. Although Patti was upset by our presence, she showed no animosity to us at all. In fact, we awaited the return of Harrison while listening to music, which was very nice. Harrison returned with his lawyer and the premises was searched. Various amounts of cannabis resin were found and I arrested both Harrison and Boyd for possession of the drug and they were conveyed to Esher police station, formally charged and later released on bail. On their appearance at a later date in court, pleas of guilty were accepted and small fines were imposed. During the course of this matter and due to a conversation I had with Harrison, I hardened my view that the policy of enforcement was not effective.

The next day, the papers were saying how we arranged the bust on 'the day Paul McCartney was getting married' on purpose and for publicity. I didn't know Paul McCartney was getting married – nor did anyone else! Perhaps if I'd have known, I'd have changed the date to ensure less press but the idea was that we did it to attract them: nonsense!

I later learned that Patti Boyd had discovered some cannabis in her car in a handbag and that Harrison had more cannabis on the premises but I was not concerned about this. He had enough problems. It was later reported by Simon Wells that the search was carried out before Harrison returned home. As mentioned, the search was in fact carried out in the presence of Harrison and his lawyer when the drugs were discovered by the dogs.

*

The other very significant factor in the development of our thinking at the Squad was the effect upon us all of having to witness the results of drug abuse. Our work wasn't all about nabbing celebrities – it was about dealing with what those drugs delivered.

For example, a year before the Harrison arrest, in the summer of 1968, I received information relating to Tubby Hayes, a top jazz saxophonist, that he was into the misuse of drugs and in a very serious way. I knew of Tubby and his reputation in the music world as being the great saxophonist and it seemed he was in fact in grave danger with some very serious medical problems due to him overusing cannabis. I decided to look into Tubby's situation and a search was carried out which confirmed that he was drug abusing in a big way. He was really a sick man, I could see him going down the pan. As was the case with Brian Jones, we were in a position to intervene with the possession charges in an attempt to save lives. Seeing Tubby, I felt in fact that he needed urgent medical assistance and so I took him to Charing Cross Hospital in order that he could receive some key treatment.

As a result of my involvement with Hayes, I met a man who was friends with Tubby. He was the father of Hemmings, the Olympic gold medallist. This gentleman was deeply concerned with Hayes' condition, as we all were. Unfortunately our best efforts could not save Tubby from his deep-rooted addiction. He was in such a bad way and, rather than busting and charging him – as I was required – and despite his extraordinary use of cannabis, I endeavoured to get Tubby the help. Nigel and I used to check on him twice a week, meet him for a cup of coffee in a cafe near where he was living in Hans Place, just behind Harrods. If we met him at midday, he'd be in a pretty gruesome state because he wouldn't have finished at Ronnie Scott's before three in the morning, or he might have travelled back from a gig out of town. So we'd say, come on Tubby, let's have a coffee and we'd try and get some orange juice down him. But I could not help him in the end – he was being supplied by all these people in the music industry who depended on his talent: the music managers, the A&R men. They all kept supplying him and Tubby couldn't get by without it – he was addicted, end of story. He was a lovely man. And yet even Ronnie Scott himself said to me once, Norman, you're probably the best friend he's got. He died on the 8th June 1973 aged thirty-eight.

The fact of the matter was clear: marijuana was doing huge damage and although people were dying of organ failure and not marijuana use on paper, the large scale unhealthy living and use of marijuana was not helping; and it was removing some of the pain people were feeling, whilst ushering them further into negative life habits. It was killing people softly. We looked after Tubby at the end trying to get him off the drugs but he was using it to such a degree that our efforts were useless. By this time I had developed a good relationship with him, and had formed a friendship with him over a period of a few months. We were meeting each other in the odd teashop, and so of course I was going to fight for Tubby and not arrest him. I was sad that I couldn't push him hard enough to stop his drug using and it was a failure on my part.

*

Time passed after Tubby died, and investigators began to recognise much concerning the culture of the agencies. In many cases, in order to ensure successful convictions and cut the drug supply at source, it was necessary to bend the rules or even break them. These investigators knew how to research: for the negative culture that pervades the service is the result of decades of brainwashing, carried out by senior officers and 'you do whatever needs to be done to obtain results' was its maxim. This toxic and dangerous culture was endemic throughout all of the enforcement agencies including MI5, MI6, Customs and Excise and the police service, initially encouraged by senior staff in the police as they rely on successful results to ensure their own progress in the service. It is well documented that where there were questions of wrongdoing, the first response was to act by forming special squads to investigate a matter; but the problem was and always has been that these squads were mainly staffed by officers who were normally as bad, or worse, than those they were appointed to investigate. The corrupt fixing the corrupt! The result was usually that no action could ever be taken. Instead, the virus would spread and as more men allowed themselves to become compromised, the sicker the culture became, until it degenerated into a level of corruption that was lost in its own dishonesty. In an attempt to help cut the drugs at the source, I was required to understand the culture of corruption in a deep way, and the death of Tubby drove me forward, as well as the mess others found themselves in due to a sick and irresponsible relationship with marijuana and LSD.

It is true to say that the culture of corruption within the service reached wild and recalcitrant levels that were totally unmanageable. This began in the late '70s and ran through the decades into around 2000. There have been a number of books published which allege the reality of what I am alluding to but to observe such corruption go unchallenged by those in power has been very difficult to fathom. Politicians wring their hands and pontificate about dealing with these matters to no end. They have always been, one might say, 'aware' of the negative situation while they rely on the actions of the police to deal in crime. Running around as an officer arresting the common man for drugs charges was a waste of my time and that of my unit, when the source of the issue was allowed to run wild; through corrupt high-powered persons, I believe that it was encouraged to continue.

Politicians were also well aware that crime figures were toyed with in order to present a certain ideal: namely, to give the impression that crime was under control. The fact was and still is that if reported crimes were collated truthfully, there would be a period of great recrimination amongst those in power, and it would lead to a transparency, which is sorely needed, including in the actions of the police service. If transparency was encouraged, the wicked behaviour of powerful people self-protecting to save their own skins would be highlighted and many such people all the way down to the bent officer would face great scrutiny and exposure. It was a paradox therefore that men in my unit were required to face such scrutiny and this paradox was a reflection of the corrupting and framing practises of peoples' motive to save face, hide and play the coward.

My father's desire for me, by demonstration, to show right and honest behaviour, to work an honest day, was the reason I joined the police, not to arrest pop stars or entertain the sick ways of powerful men. I saw many men who began with good solid intentions, and gradually through temptation and fear, succumbed to the impulses of money – and many men were frightened into corruption in a kind of 'you scratch my back' way. Succumbing to such fears seemed to perpetuate the corruption, and yet I was the one who was destined for prison. The scathing of my reputation and that of my unit only reinforced the truth of the pervading corruption that was extensive throughout the force, all the way up the ranks into the echelons where cowardly and nasty people were prepared to save face and avoid humiliation. They would do anything to avoid prison. Sometimes it was very small actions – 'Cutting off the nose to spite the face' – that would generate chaos, all of which led to good (perhaps naïve) men being left to take the fall when their intention was to follow protocol, clock off and return home to their families, sleep a good night and then get up and work.

During a period of continual work, which was showing no reduction in demands on the unit's time, I spoke to Detective Superintendent Jim Barnett, our boss, who we rarely saw because of his other commitments, and I discussed with him the growing problems we had with the leaking of information out of our office. He agreed and he was aware of the situation and had in fact been watching the position closely. We discussed the various avenues whereby the information was being passed out of the office and we came to the conclusion that one particular officer was responsible and that Jim Barnett would deal with the matter, which he did, resulting in an officer being transferred out of the department. 'The only thing necessary for the triumph of evil is for good men to do nothing,' the saying goes, and there was little point scratching my head. Furthermore, I was becoming sick of the corruption, tired of it and I did not wish to lose hope. There was no point moaning about things. I had seen success for the team now that the officer had been transferred out and so I took another step forward. I began to discuss the constant interference in our cases mainly by senior officers outside of C1. Superintendent Barnett advised me that if I was aware of anybody being connected with the Freemasons, I should not become involved or upset them if I was looking to seek further promotion. I had identified the group responsible and knew now who was playing gatekeeper. It was as it always has been… the Lodge.

As a result of information passed on to Vic Kelaher by BNDD (the American Bureau of Narcotics and Dangerous Drugs) agents, the entire squad was involved in a case where a contact from the USA was arranging for large supplies of LSD to be imported into the UK. It was clear that a number of telephones were being monitored which required observations to be kept on a number of suspects throughout Greater London. The build-up of evidence reached a stage where we decided that action had become necessary.

A number of teams were nominated to affect the search and arrest procedure. A coordinated number of searches were arranged at a specified time. The team I lead kept observation on three suspects, who were meeting in the Silver Lounge, a restaurant in Leicester Square. At the agreed time we stepped in and arrested the men who we believed to be the prime movers in this case. It had been prearranged that any persons arrested would be taken to a number of selected police stations and as a result of this operation a total of nine men were detained and charged with conspiracy offences. The nine men appeared at Bow Street Magistrates Court and I appeared as the arresting officer. I requested that they all be remanded in custody due to the serious nature of the charges and mentioned the danger of a flight risk. One of the suspects was a US National suspected of being involved in serious crimes in the US. The magistrate granted my request and they were all remanded in custody for seven days.

I returned to our office to complete the required paperwork and continue with the enquiries requested by the prosecution. In the course of that week I was approached by one of our detective inspectors who said that on my return to court to follow up the case I was not to object to bail in relation to the US National. I asked him where this instruction had originated from and he stated that Commander Gerrard, the officer in charge of operations for the CID, had passed it on to him. I made it very clear that I had no intention of carrying out the order and that if he wished to nominate another officer to take over this matter then 'good luck'. I was very angry about the entire situation because we all built up a level of credibility when appearing before the magistrates and I had no intention of that being questioned.

I was being followed and that same evening whilst I was in the underground car park, I was approached by a civilian driver, who drove Commander Gerrard's car. He told me that he knew I was involved in this case and that I had known him for a number of years. I confirmed that fact and he told me that the previous evening Gerrard had ordered him to drive to Soho Square at a specific time and to drive slowly around the square with his rear window lowered. This of course he did and a small package was thrown into the car through the open window. This package he later handed to Gerrard. What the package contained remains a matter of conjecture although I have always had my own opinion in view of the earlier events in this case.

*

A request was made by the Foreign and Commonwealth Office to New Scotland Yard for a senior officer to travel to the Cayman Islands in order to prepare a report on the reorganisation of the police service there. Detective Superintendent Jim Barnett was nominated to carry out this request. Fortunately, I was informed that I would assist Mr Barnett in this work at his request and that I would be away for several weeks. I was very happy with the knowledge that I would be able to see at first-hand how Mr Barnett worked. I was not concerned that I was leaving current cases in abeyance because I knew that the team were more than capable of handling the cases under enquiry.

We travelled to Grand Cayman via Miami where we spent two days, which allowed me to look at the way the BNDD agents dealt with the very serious problems they had. There had been a large raid organised which we were invited to observe. It was obvious that the very visible amount of firearms on view confirmed that these raids were violent incidents; something that we were luckily not familiar with. Both Jim and I were content that our problems at home did not compare to those we witnessed in Miami. On our arrival in Grand Cayman we were welcomed by the Administrator who was in charge on the islands. We stayed at what was then the Beach Club in idyllic conditions. In 1970 the islands had not been developed to any extent, but I guessed at the time that plans were in hand to make the islands into a financial centre. The blue waters of the Caribbean were quite a calming and serene change from London, the commute and the hard graft of the smoke. Unfortunately we were not here on holiday and had a job to do.

We assessed the lay of the land regarding the effectiveness of the police force, which was supervised by the typical ex-pat – who was never expected to be conversant with up-to-date police practices. As a small example: Jim and I were leaving the Administrator's office one morning and as we waited to exit the main gate onto the main road we saw a Mini Moke car coming from our right on the wrong side of the road. Travelling from our left we saw a Ford Consul on the correct side of the road. We could only watch, in slow motion, as the cars collided head on. The man and woman in the Mini Moke were thrown over the Ford, which was very seriously damaged. I attended to the female passenger, whilst Jim dealt with the man, both of whom were middle aged. I could not assist the woman who died within a short period and unfortunately Jim fared no better as the man also died. The car driver was not seriously injured but another car passed by – the driver speeding away. We managed to call for assistance, which arrived in the form of four constables on the back of a lorry. In the meantime we were told that the car which had sped past us had hit a tree further along the road. When we checked that out we found that the driver was also dead. As I expected, Jim took control of the situation and we finished up dealing with the subsequent paperwork. To have a person die in your own arms is a dreadful thing, they were Americans who had come over on their holiday, sadly never to return. It was moments like these that were truly harrowing as events but they were part of the job and we were to take full responsibility when they would occur and always do our best to remain calm and collected through them as servants to the public.

During our work I realised just how good Jim Barnett was at his job, completely in charge of situations and very decisive in a capable way. It was a trait that I had found to be missing in a lot of senior officers. In fact during our discussions he advised me to be careful in my dealings with certain officers. During the course of this trip I had learned a good deal from Jim of the culture in New Scotland Yard and how it operated. He advised me to stay clear of Masons and in particular a quango of senor officers within C1. It was this trip to Cayman where I confirmed my own views: that there was indeed a group of senior officers who were not averse at all to acting in a manner that was entirely corrupt, and not in a loose and general way, but in a real and malevolent way. With the distance I had from London and in light of this new information, it all in fact, made complete sense. We flew back home.

On my return to the office I found that the team had carried on and completed a large number of enquiries. A downside was that information regarding our work was still being leaked. As a result of undercover work by Nick Prichard he had contacted a dealer who had large amounts of cannabis resin for sale. A meeting had been arranged in the West End, which I decided to cover in case of problems so I booked out a nondescript observation van and kept in contact with Nick by radio. After some time waiting in Hyde Park I received a call from Nick that the dealer had agreed a sale of nine weights of resin, which he had in the boot of a sports car. Nick had arranged to meet the dealer, who was on his way to Kensington to meet his supplier, with the required cash later. I was on Hyde Park Corner and saw the sports car heading towards Knightsbridge so I radioed for assistance, as I could not identify the hired van as a police vehicle. I received a response from a traffic patrol car, which stopped the sports car in Knightsbridge. The result of this stop was that I found a parcel in the car boot which did in fact contain nine weights of resin, so I arrested the man who was taken to Hyde Park Police Station where I later questioned him. He admitted that he was attempting to sell the resin, which had been supplied to him by a family named Salah. He also admitted that he had been moving large quantities of the drug on behalf of the Salah family who were planning to import a further shipment into the UK. He agreed to pass me any information he could obtain in relation to this family's activities and this was the type of information I wanted. Rather than take interest in petty crime, I was now able to attack the supply chain. He was charged and later dealt with at Quarter Sessions. The Salah saga had just begun.

At this point myself, Nigel, Nick, Adam and Morag were making countless arrests and we were working round the clock. We'd meet up in the morning at the coffee shop, then go into the office and discuss what we were going to do and then look at the lists of jobs that we had. I'd then go to Bow Street and get the warrants and we'd go out and spend the day searching properties and it would be half a dozen a day... some successful, some not. We were working our socks off and at the end of the day, when we looked down at the amount of drugs we had taken off the streets, it was laughable compared to the amount that was going around. I had a think about things over a period of days, and more time to reflect on what happened to Tubby, as well as the corruption within the Met that Jim shared with me in the Cayman Islands. I got the team together and we had a talk in the yard. It was to be the defining whisper amongst us.

'I still think what we're doing is not in our remit. I guess we're all a bit tired of this and especially the nonsense we're getting from the press. So, I'm thinking – maybe we should slow down with all the small ones and concentrate now only on the big ones.'

It was nods all round. They were much needed words. I was simply saying what everyone knew.

'It might take us more time to cover and investigate but we'd be removing tons of cannabis or thousands of acid tablets and that idea seems more satisfying and helpful than all this messing around.' There was silence in the yard but I spoke on. 'What do you think men? Shall we try harder? To go after the dealers?'

But there was someone who was destined to stop us. That someone was Robert Mark.

When I was posted to New Scotland Yard, Robert Mark had also arrived, having been appointed as an Assistant Commissioner at the behest of Roy Jenkins – the Home Secretary at the time. Everything changed. In an attempt to root out the corruption, good men were to be used as pawns, collateral where the end of his ambition justified the means of his actions.

Chapter 8
Robert Mark

Mark was born in 1917 and after a grammar school education he eventually joined the Manchester City police in '37. He was appointed to the Special Branch in '38 and served there until 1942 when he joined the Armoured Corp serving throughout Europe. Mark remained in Germany with the Control Commission with the rank of Major until 1947. On his return to Manchester he again worked in Special Branch. In 1950 he was promoted to Inspector until he was again promoted to Chief Inspector in uniform in 1952. It was clear that Mark was a vastly experienced police officer with ambitions to reach the top in the service and it was this combination of ambition and competence that would always lead to 'success' as it has come to be known. And if success meant a high-ranking position, Mark was about to become a success.

This success was borne out by the fact that at the young age of thirty-nine years, Mark was appointed as the Chief Constable of Leicester. During the next ten years he set out to raise his personal profile and then a rare opportunity came his way when Lord Mountbatten made it known that he required an assistant in drawing up a report relating to prison security, in particular the escape of George Blake from Wormwood Scrubs prison. There was no doubt that Mark was a very shrewd individual who would have surely realised that to gain the confidence of a person such as Mountbatten was an opportunity not to be missed. Mark's meeting with Mountbatten certainly pushed him forward into the Met. Had they not met, I doubt that he would have become Commissioner. At the conclusion of the Mountbatten enquiry, Mark reappeared in police circles having become closely involved in politics, as a result of which he was appointed as an assistant commissioner at New Scotland Yard, again at the behest of Roy Jenkins, the Home Secretary. Mark had at last worked his way into the closed shop, commonly known as New Scotland Yard.

Shortly after Mark's arrival at the Yard, the in-post Commissioner Sir

Joseph Simpson died and this enabled James Callaghan to offer the position to Mark who realised that such a move would alienate the hierarchy at New Scotland Yard. Mark declined and suggested that he be appointed as Deputy Commissioner and that John Waldron be moved up to the position of Commissioner. The ACC (Assistant Commissioner of Crime) Peter Brodie, who had been regarded as the favourite to become Commissioner, was side-lined into another position.

On his appointment as Deputy Commissioner, Mark set about his quest to deal with the alleged corruption within CID in the Met and he initiated a policy of moving CID into uniform and vice versa. This policy was a cause for concern among career detectives who rightly felt that the service was losing the experience required to deal with crime in general. My own opinion was that the arrival of Mark was a breath of fresh air into the Met and that his declaration to deal with the alleged corrupt practices endemic within the CID was welcome; but unfortunately, Mark had introduced politics to the police service. My desires for his arrival to be in our best interests were to be disappointed, gradually but inevitably…

In 1972 Mark was appointed as Commissioner, once again confirming his intention to stamp out the alleged corruption within the CID. During my stint at New Scotland Yard it was clear that there was an element of corrupt practice which was evident, especially within the so-called specialist squads in the Met and it was also clear to me that such corruption was endemic within the higher levels of the uniform departments.

It has been claimed that the actions taken by Mark's policy resulted in the dismissal of some 487 detectives, some of whom were required to resign, but it is also clear that large numbers of detectives, some of whom were senior officers with impeccable records, sought early retirement, unwilling to serve in a service that had become so seriously politicised.

The feeling within our department was that Mark had lost his determination to concentrate on dealing with key issues, such as the influence of Freemasonry within the service and public office in general. Someone was clearly not happy with him, or perhaps he had hit the Freemason wall. There had and has been for many years a situation whereby a cancer-like spread of the unhealthiest would tempt, seduce and influence men to make decisions which diverted them from their moral compass – and the source location of this rot all seemed to emanate from a single source. It has always been the case that in order to progress within the police service, as with other public bodies, it was advisable to become a Freemason, a secret society that should play no part in the desire to work responsibly as an officer. There was an urgent need to oversee the influence of Freemasonry, which is where all our efforts should have been focused. Any person employed in a public service should therefore, by default be required to register any membership of a secret society.

It was obvious that actions to deal with this would be both difficult and complex as the people who would make any decisions to restrict such influence were likely to be Masons themselves. The influence of Freemasonry within the Met has been well documented, showing that entire specialised units were staffed by Masons. During the period 1972–1974, Mark took particular interest in the actions of our DCI, Vic Kelaher. As a result of this, the team with whom I worked came under the spotlight and we were soon to realise just how far Mark would go to obtain the result that he wanted, which was to root Kelaher out and to become a Lord.

In 1977 Mark retired after being awarded the statutory knighthood. He did in fact fail to obtain his desire of elevation to the House of Lords and history has shown that his claim to have cleaned up corruption within the Met was unfounded, as it is well documented that corruption has maintained its grip during post-Mark years. One of several accounts of this situation is graphically outlined in *The Untouchables* by Michael Gillard and Laurie Flynn. Mark retired into relative obscurity in 1977, passing away in 2010 aged 93 years.

From my observations and having had much time to reflect, this ambition to become a Lord was his motivation from the very start and he pushed and he pushed and he pushed – always – to move upwards. As a result of his pioneering activities and his force, many men were crushed beneath his boots. When the post came up to assist Mountbatten in the Blake enquiry, nobody wanted to carry the bag for that but Mark jumped in, because he knew that if he got in with Mountbatten, he would be able to influence the police and policy. This is exactly what happened and he was in no time the Assistant Commissioner in the Yard. If you think about it, to go from being Chief Constable of Leicestershire with a force of one thousand officers, to Assistant Chief Constable to Assistant to the Commissioner in the Met with 32,000 officers as he did was unbelievable. But this was stage one. When they offered him the job as Commissioner, he said he didn't want to do that because he felt that if he was suddenly appointed Commissioner, it would be viewed badly by the clan at the Yard (The Firm as they call them). He turned it down to become Deputy so he could appoint the Commissioner himself, so he was right in with the politicians. It was strategy, it was ambition, and it worked.

These people don't stop. If they could have it their way, they'd be King of the world. He was very shrewd indeed and when the then Commissioner died, he was in straight away and came in as Commissioner. This personal private agenda to become a Lord self-generated corruption and Mark was corrupt but in a different way. He was corrupt in a shrewd and even intimidating way. When he became Deputy Commissioner of the Yard, he took over the discipline within the force and he hated the Met CID – with a vengeance. He held a famous meeting of CID officers when he told them that he thought they were all corrupt. I can't believe to this day that those good officers stood there and took that because there were some damn good officers there, and they worked their socks off for the job, and they would never bend the rules in their life but they sat there and took it. I couldn't quite believe it and this was the ability Mark held. He was certainly a force.

Mark as I said was corrupt in a different way but unusually enough, he was not a Freemason. The power of Freemasonry within all public services is very strong, it is very influential indeed and Mark should have been committed to exposing that, in my view. In something like the Civil Service, Masonry doesn't matter so much but within the enforcement services, it really does. Whenever there was a 'big' job, in any of these services, they were there. They were present but invisible.

Part of Mark's mission was to take out my boss, Vic Kelaher. When Mark came in, he began to root out the corruption in the CID and they thought at the time that about 300 officers resigned, but they weren't resigning because they were corrupt. They were resigning because they couldn't work under him. They couldn't work under his rule where they would return to uniform and interchange in this fashion. They were professional investigators, now required under Mark's rule to become regular bobbies. It wasn't going to happen. It was his way of eroding their integrity and a man like Mark needed to do that to maintain his position as boss, and shatter the souls of good men to do it. Rather than have their dignity corroded, they chose to walk away, and who could blame them?

Kelaher was however, corrupt in every breath he took, keeping himself involved with villains; he was also importing cannabis. Kelaher wanted to become a senior officer in the national Drugs Squad but despite this being on the cards, none of us knew this at the time. Customs did arrest him at one stage so it was clear to Mark that he was bent out of shape, but they let him go and in doing so established the motive Mark needed to bring Kelaher to justice, no matter what. Sadly, that meant that those working under Kelaher – Morag, Nigel, Nick, Adam and myself included – would need to go to prison.

In these early days, you see, the attitude to the security of the drugs which we had impounded was very casual. When we started gathering large quantities of substances, Nigel Lilley and myself pushed for secure cabinets with coded locks in order to solve the problem of drugs going missing. Then we started our own system where we would put a small mark on our seized cannabis blocks. On one occasion, a block of cannabis resin went missing from the cabinet and it later reappeared in a search made by another unit. I knew it was the same block because it had our secret marking on it. But I couldn't take the matter any further because it would have caused serious problems for the officer involved at the time. I just took possession of the cannabis block and returned it to our secure care. And once a case was concluded, all the drugs we seized were taken to Chalk Farm for destruction.

That's just how it was. We knew that we were straight but we were constantly battling against corrupt forces inside our own organisation.

It was a good thing that Mark chose to go after Kelaher but what he should have done was leave us out of it, or get his facts straight. We were collateral damage and Mark was coming for us all. How was he going to do it? By attacking Vic Kelaher.

Norman Pilcher behind the wheel in Tripoli. © Norman Pilcher

DS Norman Pilcher having words with a cyclist

A young DC Nigel Lilley
© Nigel Lilley

Edwin Bush 21 leaving Bow Street
Magistrates Court, escorted by two
officers. DS Norman Pilcher is on
the right. Bush was charged with the
murder of 59 year old Elsie Batten. He
was later sentenced to death on 12th
May 1961 at the Old Bailey
© Mirrorpix.

Welcome to London-Savile Row

Taylor Coulson of Savile Row have built a reputation for quality clothes, impeccably tailored at prices unheard of in Savile Row.

And now, even more incredible, a suit with the distinctive line and cut of Savile Row for as little as £52.45
(exclusive p. tax)

Nigel modelling for Taylor Coulson Saville Row. © Nigel Lilley

Courtfield road drug bust 1967, Brian Jones already in the unmarked car. Norman Pilcher can be seen holding the car door open for 'Stash'.

George Harrison arrested at his home in Esher on 12th March 1969 by DS Norman Pilcher. DC Ron Spiers is on the left. © Getty Images

John Lennon being arrested at 34 Montagu Square on October 18th 1968 by DS Norman Pilcher. DS Eric Goddard is on the right.
© Getty Images

DS George Prichard leaving the Guildhall Magistrates Court after being remanded on bail in the drugs squad conspiracy case 22nd January 1973. The charges relate to the evidence given at the Salah trial the year before. He along with DC Nigel Lilley were sentenced on the 14th November 1973 at the Old Bailey to 18 months in prison.
© Getty Images

Morag McGibbon on her way to the Guildhall Magistrates Court accused of conspiracy to pervert the course of justice and perjury along with four other colleagues on 22nd January 1973. The charges relate to the evidence given at the Salah trial the year before. She was later acquitted at the Old Bailey on the 14th November 1973. © Mirrorpix

DC Nigel Lilley (left) and DC Adam Acworth, leaving Guildhall Magistrates Court after being remanded on bail on charges of conspiracy to pervert the course of justice and perjury on 22nd January 1973. The charges relate to the evidence given at the Salah trial the year before. On the 14th November 1973 at the Old Bailey Acworth was acquitted. DC Nigel Lilley was sentenced to 18 months in prison. © Unknown

Chief Inspector Vic Kelaher and DS Norman Pilcher on their way to Drug conspiracy trial at the Old Bailey on the 14th November 1973. Kelaher was acquitted while DS Norman Pilcher was found guilty of perjury and sentenced to 4 years in prison. © Mirrorpix

Judge Melford-Stevenson had only these words to say to DS Norman Pilcher before sentencing him to 4 years in prison for perjury, on the 14th November 1973. "You poisoned the wells of criminal justice and you set about it deliberately", © Getty Images

Sir Robert Mark Presenting his annual report for 1973. © Mirrorpix

Former Police Commander Wally Virgo who retired in 1973 is arrested at his home in Ledbury Herefordshire, on 27th February 1976 over bribe allegations within the Porn Squad. © Mirrorpix

Wally Virgo on his way to Bow Street Magistrates Court on the 1st March 1976 to face charges of corruption due to the evidence given by Soho Sex Club boss. Virgo was jailed in 1977. © Getty Images

Wally Virgo walks free from Leyhill Open Prison Gloucestershire, after only serving 10 months of his 12 year sentence. 15th March 1978 © Mirrorpix

Norman Pilcher 2020 © FTMB Ltd

Norman 2020 © FTMB Ltd

Norman © FTMB Ltd

**Our best endeavours have been made to locate the copyright holder(s)
FTMB LTD**

M. J. Macoun, Esq. C.M.G, O.B.E,
Foreign & Commonwealth Office,
London,
S.W.1.

35

OPA 5   F.2
                                    CR 216/70/126

8 September 1970.

Dear Macoun

DETECTIVE CHIEF SUPERINTENDENT J BARNETT
DETECTIVE SERGEANT (2nd Class) PILCHER

I refer to previous correspondence about the release of the above
Metropolitan Police officers for a period of service in the Cayman
Islands.   Relevant financial points to be considered are set out
below.

1.   The appointments will be under the Overseas Service Act, 1958,
and the officers will require contracts from you showing their
conditions of service.   We shall require to be consulted about
these beforehand so that we can advise the officers upon any matters
on which they may look to us for guidance.

2.   Upon transfer, transfer values will be payable from the
Metropolitan Police Fund representing the capitalised value of
pensions at that time.   Similarly, when reversion to this force
takes place at the end of the contract, transfer values to take
account of additional service and any revisions in pensionable pay
will be payable to the Metropolitan Police.   This seems a little
cumbersome and it would appear reasonable to calculate the net
transfer values payable at the end of the contracts, if you can
agree to this simplification.   In the event of injury or death to
either officer during service with you, you would be responsible
for paying the award to which he was entitled under the Police
Pension Regulations, 1966, but the Metropolitan Police would in that
case be required to pay the transfer value due on the date he left
their service.

3.   Details of each officer's present pay and allowances are set
out below.   The amounts shown for the Chief Superintendent are
for each calendar month, and those for the Sergeant are for each
four weeks.

	Chief Superintendent Barnett	Sergeant Pilcher
1. Salary	£274. 11. 8d.	£127. 5. 8d.
2. Undermanning allowance	-	4.19. 8d.
3. Plain clothes and boot allowances	4. 17.11d.	5.17. 0d.
4. Rent allowance	36. 10. 0d.	32. 2. 0d.
5. Detective allowances	-	33. 2. 4d.
6. Additional rest day working	-	25.12. 9d.

80

- 2 -

From all items except 3, are deducted the normal PAYE income tax, National Insurance and Graduated Pension Contributions, and various local payments to clubs, etc. Pension contributions are also deducted; these amount to £19-0-10, per month for Barnett and £7-14-5, per four weeks for Pilcher. I would assume that when settling pay arrangements, you would take account of items 1 - 5 above, but would ignore 6 on the ground that Pilcher would be compensated for loss of this item by the special honorarium you no doubt intend to pay.

4.   In May each year officers are paid a compensatory grant, which is a payment equal to the amounts they have paid in income tax on rent allowance received during the year, and in income tax paid on the previous year's compensatory grant. The payments made to Barnett and Pilcher under this head in May 1970 were £177-16-0, and £184-3-0, respectively; we would, of course, include a proportionate part of these sums in the claim.

5.   All items on the claim except the net transfer value will be subject to our normal 15% departmental charge.

6.   As in the case of other transfers recently arranged, the mechanics of each officer's emoluments, i.e. payment into their bank accounts, will continue to be dealt with from this Office if you wish.

7.   It will be for you to arrange the booking of air passages and the provision of any special clothing considered necessary.

8.   We should like the earliest possible notification of the date the officers will return.

Yours sincerely,

J L DAVIES

19th January 1971.

Thank you very much for your letter of
14th January expressing your appreciation and
that of the Administrator of the Cayman Islands
of the manner in which Detective Chief
Superintendent Barnett and Detective Sergeant
Pilcher carried out their enquiry into ganja
(cannabis) abuse in the Cayman Islands. I am
sure the officers concerned will be as pleased
as I am to hear of your kind remarks.

The cordial hospitality extended to
Detective Chief Superintendent Barnett and
Detective Sergeant Pilcher by the Administrator
of the Cayman Islands and the co-operation of
his senior staff greatly assisted the officers
in this delicate assignment.

Yours sincerely,

D.A. Scott, Esq., C.M.G.

Foreign and Commonwealth Office

London S.W.1

14 January 1971

Sir John Waldron, KCVO.
Commissioner,
Metropolitan Police Headquarters,
New Scotland Yard,
London, SW1.

My dear Commissioner

      I have read with great interest the report of
Detective Chief Superintendent Barnett and Detective
Sergeant Pilcher on their enquiry into ganja (cannabis)
abuse in the Cayman Islands, and I would like to express
our warm appreciation of the efficient and painstaking
manner with which these Officers carried out the
assignment.

      I know that the Administrator of the Cayman
Islands would wish to be included in this expression of
thanks, not only because your officers have produced such
a valuable report, but also because they clearly understood and took into account the political and social
difficulties which are prevalent in these small islands.
I am sure in particular that the statement made to the
local press in the Cayman Islands will have been invaluable
in killing some of the baseless and harmful rumours which
have been circulating there.

D A SCOTT

THE   QUEEN

against

NORMAN CLEMENCE PILCHER,

GEORGE NICHOLAS PRICHARD
and

NIGEL PATRICK STURGESS LILLEY

COPY/NOTICE AND GROUNDS OF APPEAL

(PILCHER)

D of P.P.

CRIMINAL APPEAL ACT, 1968

COURT OF APPEAL
CRIMINAL DIVISION

Grounds of Application for
Extension of Time
Leave to Appeal Against Conviction
Leave to Appeal Against Sentence

REF. No. 5365.6.73

FULL NAMES OF APPELLANT
Block Letters

FORENAMES
NORMAN CLEMENCE

SURNAME
PILCHER

Give the Name and Address of the Solicitor and/or Counsel (if any) who represented the Appellant at the Trial

SOLICITOR
Kingsley Napley & Co.
Rolls Chambers, Star Yard,
Carey Street, WC2A 2JW

COUNSEL
Mr. S. Shields
10 Kings Bench Walk, & 3 Kings
Temple, EC4

THE APPLICATIONS ARE FOR:—

LEAVE TO APPEAL AGAINST CONVICTION for the following offences:—

See below

LEAVE TO APPEAL AGAINST THE FOLLOWING SENTENCES OR ORDERS:—

See below

THE GROUNDS ARE AS FOLLOWS:— (Include reasons for delay if extension asked for)

GROUNDS OF APPEAL AGAINST CONVICTION

It is respectfully submitted that the Learned Judge was wrong in law in allowing the Crown to adduce the evidence of Mrs. Oddy after the case for the Crown had closed and also the cases for the Appellants Pilcher and Lilley had closed in that

(1) the evidence did not arise ex improviso, in that the existence of Mrs. Oddy was known to the prosecution from the time that witness

I HAVE READ FORM AA

(Signed) Solicitor (Appellant)

Date 10/12/73

Address of person signing on behalf of Appellant (See Note 13)
Rolls Chambers, Star Yard,
Carey Street, London, WC2A 2JW

© National Archives Kew

Page 3

statements were obtained from the Officers of H.M. Customs and Excise (Mr. Hanaford and Mr. Cockerell) and her importance as a witness was apparent from the time the Appellant Lilley gave evidence at the trial of the Salahs that he had left Mrs. Oddy's house before 9.a.m. on the morning of 19th January 1971.

(2) nor did the evidence fall within any exception to the general principle that evidence for the prosecution should be called during the case for the prosecution.

GROUNDS OF APPEAL AGAINST SENTENCE

In all the circumstances, especially the Jury's rider, it is respectfully submitted that a sentence of 4 years imprisonment was excessive.

Continue (and sign) on Page 4 if necessary.

I HAVE READ FORM A.A	Date		SEE NOTE B
(Signed) Solicitor (Appellant)	10/12/7	G	

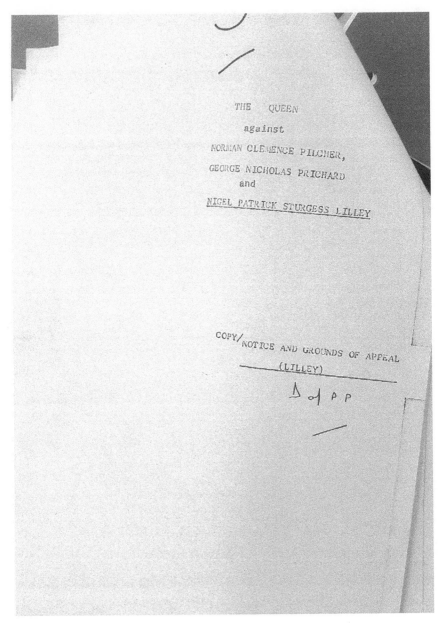

THE QUEEN

against

NORMAN CLEMENCE PILCHER,

GEORGE NICHOLAS PRICHARD
and

NIGEL PATRICK STURGESS LILLEY

COPY/NOTICE AND GROUNDS OF APPEAL

(LILLEY)

CRIMINAL APPEAL ACT, 1968

| COURT OF APPEAL CRIMINAL DIVISION | Grounds of Application for Extension of Time Leave to Appeal Against Conviction Leave to Appeal Against Sentence | To the Registrar, Criminal Appeal O... REF. No. 53 ... |

Write Legibly in Black

FULL NAMES OF APPELLANT
Block letters

| | FORENAMES | SURNAME |
| | NIGEL PATRICK STURGESS | LILLEY |

Give the Name and Address of the Solicitor and/or Counsel (if any) who represented the Appellant at the Trial

SOLICITOR Kingsley Napley & Co.
Rolls Chambers, Star Yard,
Carey Street, ...

COUNSEL Mr. K. Parker & Mr. C. ...
6 Pump Court,
Temple, EC4

List of Documents sent with this Form which the Appellant wishes to be returned. Criminal Appeal Forms will NOT be returned

THE APPLICATIONS ARE FOR:—

EXTENSION of time in which to give notice of application for leave to appeal against:—

*CONVICTION and *SENTENCE
(*Delete if inapplicable)

LEAVE TO APPEAL AGAINST CONVICTION for the following offences:—

See below

LEAVE TO APPEAL AGAINST THE FOLLOWING SENTENCES OR ORDERS:—

See below

THE GROUNDS ARE AS FOLLOWS:— (Include reasons for delay if extension asked for)

If Grounds of Appeal have been settled and signed by Counsel they should be sent with this Form (see note 13)

GROUNDS OF APPEAL AGAINST CONVICTION

1.   It is respectfully submitted that the Learned Judge was wrong in law in allowing the Crown to adduce the evidence of Mrs. Oddy after the case for the Crown had closed and also the cases for the Appellants Pilcher and Lilley had closed in that

(1) the evidence did not arise ex improviso, in that the existence of Mrs. Oddy was known to the prosecution from the time that witness

Continue (if signed) on Page 3 if necessary.

I HAVE READ FORM AA

(Signed) ... Solicitor (Appellant)

Date 10/12/73

Address of person signing on behalf of Appellant (See Note 13)
Rolls Chambers, Star Yard,
Carey Street, London, WC2A 2...

FOR USE IN THE CRIMINAL APPEAL
Received   ... DEC 1973
RECEIVED

Form 1197 51430—1-5-73 XBD

© National Archives Kew

statements were obtained from the Officers of H.M. Customs and Excise
(Mr. Hansford and Mr. Cockerell) and her importance as a witness was
apparent from the time the Appellant Lilley gave evidence at the trial
of the Salahs that he had left Mrs. Oddy's house before 9.am on the
morning of 19th January 1971.

(2) nor did the evidence fall within any exception to the general
principle that evidence for the prosecution should be called during
the case for the prosecution.

2. It is respectfully submitted that the Jury's verdict of Guilty on
Count 8 was unreasonable for the following reasons:

(a) By acquitting Acworth and McGibbon completely, the Jury
rejected the Prosecution's contention that they did not keep the
observations that were noted in their pocket books, despite the
inconsistent entries in their duty books and diaries.

(b) By acquitting Lilley on Count 11, the Jury rejected the
Prosecutions contention that he did not keep the observation of 26th
February 1971, despite the discrepancy between his pocket book and his
duty book and diary entries, and consequently were not satisfied that
his pocket book entry, made on that date, was false.

(c) By acquitting all Defendants of Count 12, the Jury accepted
that the above discrepancies could have arisen as a result of a
falsification direction given by Kelaher and/or Pilcher on the ground
of security.

(d) The Jury's conviction on Count 8, therefore, must have been
on the basis that there was an individual agreement between Pilcher
and Lilley to manufacture the observation of 19th January 1971 and
falsely enter a note of the same in their pocket books, although the
possibility of such a separate and special agreement never formed part
of the Prosecution's case.

(e) The Jury's verdict on Count 8 ignored the following undisputed
evidence:

(1) The need to manufacture evidence would not have arisen until
19th March 1971 when the Drugs Squad became aware that it would not be
possible to arrest the Salahs within the Jurisdiction.

Continue (and sign) on Page 4 if necessary.

I HAVE READ FORM A.A	Date	SEE NOTE 13
Kweite, Neale & Co 10/12/73 G		
(Signed) Solicitor (Appellant)		

Page 4

(2) There was no evidence to suggest that Lilley's pocket book had in any way been tampered with or that it did not form a chronological contemporaneous record of the matters entered in it.

(3) Following the note of the observation of 19th January 1971, in the pocket book were notes of observations of 20th and 21st January 1971, which by their verdicts the Jury accepted could have been kept and noted at the time, and a note of an arrest on 22nd January 1971. Thus by March 19th 1971 it would have been impossible to insert chronologically in the pocket book a manufactured observation relating to 19th January 1971.

GROUNDS OF APPEAL AGAINST SENTENCE

An immediately effective sentence of 18 months imprisonment for an offence of perjury, committed by a serving Police Officer while giving evidence in a case at the Central Criminal Court, cannot be said to be wrong in principle, but was too severe in all the circumstances of this case, and in particular:-

(1) The Learned Judge did not give full effect to the rider added by the Jury when they returned their verdicts

(2) The Learned Judge did not give full effect to the fact that the Appellant, having been acquitted on Count 12, should be sentenced for an isolated act, committed after an order had been given to him (a Detective Constable) by the Detective Sergeant in charge of his squad at the instance of his Detective Chief Inspector to falsify entries in his official Diary and Duty Book

(3) The Learned Judge did not give full effect to the fact that the case for the Crown was throughout that the Appellant committed this offence as the result of an order expressed by his Detective Sergeant to make a false entry in his official Pocket Book, from which he subsequently gave evidence in the Salah Trial.

This Notice of Appeal will be amended to include references as soon as the transcript is obtained.

I HAVE READ FORM AA	Date	SEE NOTE 13	C. C. A.
[signature]	10/12/73	G	11 DEC 1973
(Signed) Solicitor (Appellant)			RECEIVED

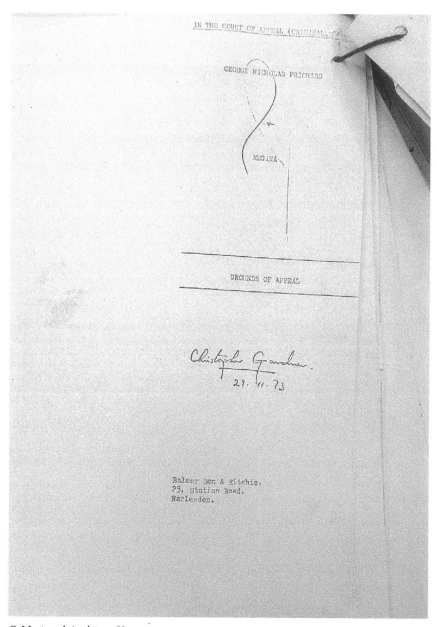

IN THE COURT OF APPEAL (CRIMINAL

GEORGE NICHOLAS PRICHARD

-v-

REGINA

GROUNDS OF APPEAL

Christopher Gardner.
29.11.73

Balmer Son & Ritchie,
25, Station Road,
Harlesden.

CRIMINAL APPEAL ACT, 1968

COURT OF APPEAL
CRIMINAL DIVISION N

NOTICE OF APPLICATION
FOR LEAVE TO APPEAL
AND OF OTHER APPLICATIONS
(See Note 7)

REF. No.

PART 1

	FULL NAMES Block letters	FORENAMES	SURNAME	Age on Conviction
Particulars of APPELLANT	ADDRESS If detained give address where detained	GEORGE NICHOLAS	PRICHARD	25
		H.M. Prison, Ford, Arundel, Sussex.	Index number if detained 126420	

COURT where tried and/or Sentenced. (see note 3)	DATES of appearances at the Court including dates of conviction (if convicted at the Court) and sentence. 17.9.73 until 14.11.73	Name of Court	Central Criminal Court
		Name of Judge	H.H. Judge MELFORD STEVENSON

Particulars of OFFENCES of which convicted.	OFFENCES	Convicted on INDICTMENT or by MAGISTRATES COURT	SENTENCES AND ORDERS
	Perjury	Ind	18 months impt.

Offences TAKEN INTO CONSIDERATION when sentenced.

TOTAL SENTENCE
18 months impt

PART 2

The appellant is applying for:— (*Delete if inapplicable)

*LEAVE to appeal against CONVICTION.

*LEAVE to appeal against SENTENCE.

*LEGAL AID.

*BAIL.

*LEAVE to be present at hearing.

Date 26.11.73   Address of person signing on behalf of Appellant
Balmer Son and Ritchie
25, Station Road, N.W.10.
Solicitors for Appellant

SEE NOTES ON BACK | CRIMINAL APPEAL ACT, 1968 | (See 112 Form 3)

| COURT OF APPEAL CRIMINAL DIVISION G | Grounds of Application for Extension of Time Leave to Appeal Against Conviction Leave to Appeal Against Sentence | To the Registrar, Criminal Appeal Office REF. No. 5091R/73 Royal Courts of Justice, Strand, London |

Write Legibly in Black

FULL NAMES OF APPELLANT
Block letters

FORENAMES: George Nicholas   SURNAME: PRICHARD

Give the Name and Address of the Solicitor and/or Counsel (if any) who represented the Appellant at the Trial

SOLICITOR: Balmer Son and Ritchie 25, Station Road, Harlesden. N.W.10.

COUNSEL: Mr. William HOWARD, Q.C. Mr. Christopher GARDNER

List of Documents sent with this Form which the Appellant wishes to be returned. Criminal Appeal Forms will NOT be returned

Nil   (Grounds of Appeal being prepared by Counsel)

THE APPLICATIONS ARE FOR:—

~~EXTENSION OF TIME IN WHICH TO MAKE THE FOLLOWING APPLICATION(S)~~

~~CONVICTIONS X SENTENCES~~
(*Delete if inapplicable)

Delete this section if no extension required

LEAVE TO APPEAL AGAINST CONVICTION for the following offences:—

Perjury

Delete this section if there is no application against conviction

LEAVE TO APPEAL AGAINST THE FOLLOWING SENTENCES OR ORDERS:—

18 months imprisonment

Delete this section if there is no application against sentence

THE GROUNDS ARE AS FOLLOWS:—(Include reasons for delay if extension asked for)
If Grounds of Appeal have been settled and signed by Counsel they should be sent with this Form (see note 14)

Grounds of Appeal are being settled by Counsel and will be forwarded when received.

Continue (and sign) on Page 3 if necessary.

I HAVE READ FORM AA

(Signed)

Date: 26.11.73

(Appellant)

Address of person signing on behalf of Appellant (See Note 14)
Balmer Son and Ritchie, Solicitors for the Appellant 25, Station Road, Harlesden, N.W.10.

FOR USE IN THE CRIMINAL APPEAL OFFICE
Received

G

Form 1457 51430—4-5-70 XBD

Messrs Kingsley Napley & Co
Solicitors
Rolls Chambers   CM/CC/A.2457
Star Yard
Carey Street   PNW/4502/72
London WC2A 2JW

                          March 1973

Dear Sir

              R v Adam Acworth, Niger Lilley
                   and Norman Pilcher

     I refer to your letter of 22nd February 1973.

     I have consulted Commander Clarkson and Commander Walton of C.2 New Scotland Yard about the requests made in your letter. I am not prepared to supply you with copies of items 1 to 8 and 10 to 18 inclusive mentioned in your letter. My reasons for these are as follows:-

          (1) all these items are of a confidential nature

          (2) the content of most of these items would appear
               to be irrelevant and immaterial to the preparation
               of your clients' defence, and

          (3) the items collectively represent a considerable amount
               of documentation, and therefore copying 'in toto' would
               be an expensive and time-consuming task.

     However, it would be possible for arrangements to be made for you and your clients to have access to certain of the items. Furthermore, if you can make your request more specific by giving details of which parts of which items you are interested in, it might then be possible to comply with your request.

                    Yours faithfully

                    W. H. WALKER

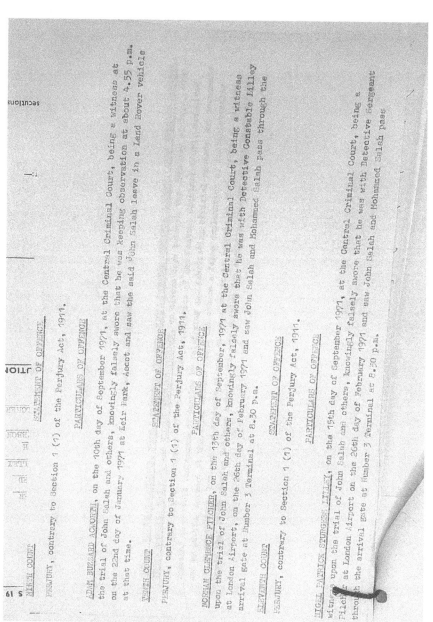

NINTH COUNT

STATEMENT OF OFFENCE

PERJURY, contrary to Section 1 (1) of the Perjury Act, 1911.

PARTICULARS OF OFFENCE

ADAM BUZZARD ACHORNE, on the 10th day of September 1971, at the Central Criminal Court, being a witness at the trial of John Salah and others, knowingly falsely swore that he was keeping observation at about 4.55 p.m. on the 22nd day of January 1971 at Keir Park, Ascot and saw the said John Salah leave in a Land Rover vehicle at that time.

TENTH COUNT

STATEMENT OF OFFENCE

PERJURY, contrary to Section 1 (1) of the Perjury Act, 1911.

PARTICULARS OF OFFENCE

NORMAN GLENWROE PILCHER, on the 13th day of September, 1971 at the Central Criminal Court, being a witness upon the trial of John Salah and others, knowingly falsely swore that he was with Detective Constable Lilley at London Airport, on the 26th day of February 1971 and saw John Salah and Mohammed Salah pass through the arrival gate at Number 3 Terminal at 8.30 p.m.

ELEVENTH COUNT

STATEMENT OF OFFENCE

PERJURY, contrary to Section 1 (1) of the Perjury Act, 1911.

PARTICULARS OF OFFENCE

NIGEL PATRICK STURGESS LILLEY, on the 15th day of September 1971, at the Central Criminal Court, being a witness upon the trial of John Salah and others, knowingly falsely swore that he was with Detective Sergeant Pilcher at London Airport on the 26th day of February 1971 and saw John Salah and Mohammed Salah pass through the arrival gate at Number 3 Terminal at 8.30 p.m.

120

113
111
108
103
98
96
94
90

37
8

TWELFTH COUNT

STATEMENT OF OFFENCE

CONSPIRACY TO PERVERT THE COURSE OF JUSTICE

PARTICULARS OF OFFENCE

GEORGE NICHOLAS PRICHARD, NORMAN CLARENCE FILCHER, NIGEL PATRICK STURGESS LILLEY, ADAM BUZZARD ACWORTH, MORAG McDONALD McGIBBON and VICTOR RICHARD KELAHER, on divers days between the 27th day of July, 1970 and the 18th day of November, 1972 within the jurisdiction of the Central Criminal Court, conspired together to pervert the course of justice by falsifying and fabricating official records and documents and by putting forward at the trial of John Saleh and others a false explanation of inconsistencies and contradictions between the evidence of some of them and their records in their Official Diaries, namely that false entries had been made in the said Dairies for security reasons on the instructions of Victor Richard Kelaher and Norman Clemence Pilcher.

METROPOLITAN POLICE   No. 153

.....Drugs.Office......... Station CO..Division

.....23rd.March,.............1971.

PRELIMINARY APPLICATION for LEGAL AID

(To be forwarded in duplicate to Registry on the day the prisoner is remanded)

Charged at....Cannon.Row.Police.............. Station on the 28th day of

.March,.................19..71.and remanded* { on bail / in custody } until...10......{ a.m. / p.m.

on the..30th....day of.....March,................., 1971.

at the..Bow.Street...............................• { Metropolitan Magistrates' Court / Magistrates' Court }

Name..Mohammed.SALAH.........Age 55yrs. C.R.O. (if known) Awaits.
    John SALAH.   26yrs C.R.O. (if known) 79305/64.
Name..Kathleen Muriel SALAH.Age.21yrs C.R.O. (if known) Awaits.

CHARGE:—

        ALL
        'Between the 1st October, 1970 and the
        20th March, 1971 did conspire together
        with Kathleen Ruth SALAH, Janet SALAH
        and other persons unknown to contravene
        the provisions of the Dangerous Drugs
        Act, 1965 within the jurisdiction of
        the Central Criminal Court.'

        Contrary to Common Law.

        D. OF P.P. DEPT
        RECEIVED
        2 5 MAR 1971
        REGISTRY

                                    P.T.O.

© National Archives Kew

No. 991A

STATEMENT OF WITNESS
(C.J. Act. 1967, ss. 2, 9; M.C. Rules, 1968, r. 58)

Statement of... John SULLIVAN

Age of Witness (if over 21 enter "over 21").... Over 21

Occupation of Witness............................... Detective Sergeant

Address and Telephone Number....................... No.1 Area Inspectorate

.... Paddington Green Police Station,'DD'

This statement,* consisting of 2 pages each signed by me, is true to the best of my knowledge and belief and I make it knowing that, if it is tendered in evidence, I shall be liable to prosecution if I have wilfully stated in it anything which I know to be false or do not believe to be true.

Dated the 5th day of February   , 19 73.

Signed .... J.Sullivan, D/S

Signature witnessed by ....

On Wednesday, 31st January 1973, at 2.45 p.m., together with Superintendent FAULKNER, I went to the Freemantle Police Station, Freemantle, Western Australia, where we saw Norman Clemence PILCHER.

Superintendent FAULKNER said to PILCHER, "I have a warrant for your arrest," and then read the warrant to PILCHER. Mr. FAULKNER then produced the extradition warrant.

PILCHER was asked by Superintendent FAULKNER if he wished to read the documents, but he declined to do so.

Superintendent FAULKNER then told PILCHER he would be arrested and taken back to England to be charged with the offences, and after being cautioned, PILCHER replied, "I am not guilty of these charges. I want you to know I am not saying anything about that or anything else between here and there."

Signed .... J.Sullivan, D/S

Signature witnessed by ....

*Delete as applicable.

P.-69-62395

89

No. 991C

STATEMENT OF WITNESS
(C.J. Act, 1967, ss. 2, 9; M.C. Rules, 1968, r. 58)

Continuation of statement of...... John SULLIVAN, D/S

On Thursday, 1st February 1973, at 1.45 p.m., at Snow Hill
Police Station, I was present when PILCHER was charged with the offence
of conspiring to pervert the course of justice, and three cases of
perjury. The charges were read over to PILCHER; he was cautioned
but made no reply.

Signed .... Signature witnessed by ....
J. Sullivan, D/S

90

STATEMENT OF WITNESS
(C.J. Act, 1967, ss. 2, 9; M.C. Rules, 1968, r. 58)

Statement of.. Norman Clemence PILCHER

Age of Witness (if over 21 enter "over 21")........ Over 21

Occupation of Witness.. Unemployed

Address and Telephone Number .... 10 Alton Close,

Bexley, Kent.

This statement,* consisting of 3 pages each signed by me, is true to the best of my knowledge and belief and I make it knowing that, if it is tendered in evidence, I shall be liable to prosecution if I have wilfully stated in it anything which I know to be false or do not believe to be true.

Dated the 5th day of   July   , 1973.

Signed .... N.C. Pilcher

Signature witnessed by J. Sullivan, D/S

In June 1971, I was posted as a Detective Sergeant to Clapham Police Station and served there until 24th July 1972, when I resigned from the force. Prior to moving to Clapham I worked at the Drug Squad, New Scotland Yard, commencing there in 1968. When I started work at the Drug Squad, I started a private notebook to keep telephone numbers and general information in respect of drugs. I would describe it as dark red wine-coloured, stiff-backed, indexed book, 6 inches by 4 inches and ruled. Also on the inside front cover there was a C.1 office stamp with my name and rank. All the writing in the book was in my handwriting. When I went to Clapham Police Station in June 1971, I took the book with me but made no further entries in it, although I referred to it.

The last time I saw the book was when I put it in with papers and exhibits of the Salahs, after doing the legal aid report in respect of the women which would have been on or about 20th October 1971

Signed N.C. Pilcher .... Signature witnessed by J. Sullivan, D/S ....
*Delete as applicable.

399

Page 2   **STATEMENT OF WITNESS**
(C.J. Act, 1967, ss. 2, 9; M.C. Rules, 1968, r. 58)

Continuation of statement of................... Norman Clemence PILCHER

As far as I can recollect, I placed the book in with the exhibits of the case.

On 20th June 1972, Mr. Faulkner came to Clapham Police Station and with him I went through all the papers and exhibits in respect of the Salahs. It was whilst doing this that I realised the book I have previously mentioned was missing. Also missing was a bank paying-in book in the name of SALAH and formed part as an exhibit.

The loss of this book, the wine-coloured indexed book, has caused me some embarrassment because I now understand that informants mentioned in the book have been arrested or harassed.

I am not prepared to mention the details of those persons.

I have no idea who may have taken this book.

I would like to add that this book also contains details of my defence in my forthcoming trial. It was not until the 10th May 1973 when I went to Paddington Police Station and was shown numerous documents that I realised that the wine-coloured indexed notebook was not in police possession as I had believed it to be up until that time.

         (signed)   N.C. Pilcher,

         (signed)   J. Sullivan, D/S.

Signed.. Signature witnessed by...........................

WEST MERCIA CONSTABULARY

A. 30

Telephone No. K. 65122

'A' .... Division

Our Ref.:- ....

Kidderminster .... Police Station

Your Ref.:- ....

2nd July 197 3

Subject: David Francis WALKER

Sir,

I refer to a telephone conversation with Superintendent FAULKNER of the No. 1 Area Inspectorate, Metropolitan Police, on Friday 29th June 1973. At 11.40a.m. on Sunday 1st July 1973, I went to 14 Prior Close, Offmore Farm Estate, Kidderminster, where I saw David Francis WALKER, security consultant. I said, "Were you serving in the C.I.D. at Clapham Police Station between the 29th April and 15th May 1972?" He replied, "Yes." I said, "A legal aid docket was taken from D.S. PILCHER's desk when he was on annual leave. This was taken to Scotland Yard. There was a note book in this docket and it is alleged this note book has been stolen. It was wine coloured. The legal aid docket was in the name of SALAH. Did you see the legal aid docket?" He replied, "No." I said, "Were you asked to send it to Scotland Yard?" He replied, "No." I said, "Did you see a coloured note book?" He replied, "No, but I must qualify this. I do know that when Sergeant PILCHER came back off leave he was very annoyed about this docket having been taken out of his desk and he did tell me that a note book was in the docket and that this note book was important to him." I said, "Will you make a statement to this effect?" and I then outlined to him how it had been suggested that this statement should begin. He said, "I am not putting all that, I will make my own." He then made a statement which I took down on a Criminal Justice Act form and he signed it.

I ask that a copy of this report, together with the attached statement be forwarded to Superintendent FAULKNER, No. 1 Area Inspectorate, Metropolitan Police Station, Paddington, London W.2.

CONFIDENTIAL

D. R. PROSSER
Detective Sergeant 32

Chief Superintendent E. A. Baker,
KIDDERMINSTER.

C.54

Statement of witness
(C. J. Act 1967, ss. 2, 9 : M.C. Rules 1968, r. 58.)

Name: David Francis WALKER

Age of Witness (if over 21 enter "over 21")   Over 21

Occupation: Security Consultant

Address: 14 Prior Close, Offmore Farm Estate, Kidderminster.

This statement (consisting of 1 pages each signed by me.) is true to the best of my knowledge and belief and I make it knowing that, if it is tendered in evidence, I shall be liable to prosecution if I have wilfully stated in it anything which I know to be false or do not believe to be true.

Dated the   1st   day of   July   19 73

Signed. David Walker

I have been asked questions regarding the existence of a note book which was in the possession of Detective Sergeant PILCHER when he served at Clapham Police Station, at the same time as I was a Detective Constable there. However I feel that the information which I have, should not be divulged without previously being interviewed by defence solicitors acting on behalf of ex Detective Sergeant PILCHER.

Signed David Walker

KINGSLEY, NAPLEY & CO.

INCORPORATING SHURMAN & CO

H. W. Walker.

DAVID NAPLEY   SIDNEY KINGSLEY, M.B.E.
JOHN CLITHEROE LL.B   LAWRENCE P. SHURMAN M.A
DENIS S. GOODWIN, M.A.
FRANCIS WEAVER   DAVID M. SPIKER, LL.B.

SOLICITORS

ROLLS CHAMBERS,
STAR YARD, CAREY STREET,
LONDON, WC2A 2JW

TELEPHONES 01-242 6551
01-405 5556

OUR REF: CM/CC/A.2457   YOUR REF: FWW/4502/72

22nd February 1973

The Director of Public Prosecutions,
12 Buckingham Gate,
London S.W.1.

Dear Sir,

<u>R -v- Adam Acworth, Nigel Lilley
and Norman Pilcher</u>

We thank you for your letter of 15th February and note what you say.

We are obliged to you for the copies of the Intercept Transcript. We are taking our Clients' instructions upon this as it may well be that there are certain other documents referred to therein that we may wish to be disclosed. We will inform you of these as soon as possible.

With regard to the second paragraph of your letter, we visited Paddington Police Station on Tuesday 20th February together with our Clients and inspected the Occurrence Books, Non-Descript Vehicles Book and Duty Book from 1st January 1970 until 10th March 1970.

It became apparent during the meeting, at which Superintendent Faulkner was present, that we would need certain items that Superintendent Faulkner was not authorised to give us. He suggested that we write to you listing these and stating our reasons for the same.

With regard to the Duty Book referred to above,

Cont/..

2.

apparently he is unauthorised to give us a copy of the complete book, not only of our Client's entries, as certain entries may refer to enquiries being carried out by Officers other than those the subject of the present charges. We feel that this reason can hardly be valid in view of the fact that we have already been supplied with copies of certain pages of the Duty Books which contain entries regarding other Officers. Our Clients have therefore instructed us to request that we receive copies of all entries in all Duty Books from 1st January 1970 until the end of October 1971. In addition to this, we have also requested Superintendent Faulkner to supply us with copies of all Diary and Pocket Book entries of our Clients covering these dates.

With regard to our request for a complete transcript of the trial of John Salah and Others, we are applying direct to the Official Shorthand Writers for these.

During the course of taking our clients details instructions upon the case in general, it has become apparent that there are several other items that our Clients feel are of great importance in assisting them in preparing their defence *and should be supplied*.

These are as follows:-

1. Drugs Squad Daily Events Book.

2. Drugs Squad Memorandum Book.

3. Drugs Squad Action Book.

4. Salah Legal Aid Report.

5. Legal Aid Report in the case of R.V. Wilkins.

6. Legal Aid Reports in the cases of Lee and Young.

7. Informant's Report in the case of Lee and Young.

8. Informant's Report in the case of Salah.

9. Detective Sergeant Pilcher's private note book which was with the docket containing all the papers in the Salah case, all of which were taken by, we understand,

3.

Superintendent Faulkner.

10. Details of commendations received by our Clients.

11. Authority to receive a copy of General Orders.

12. Assistant Commissioner of C. Department's Consolidated Instructions.

13. Commander's Memoranda.

14. Police Orders for 1971 and 1972.

15. The Report prepared by the Lancashire Constabulary into the workings of the Drug Squad.

16. The annual leave register for 1968 to 1971.

17. The Chief Superintendent's Conference Notes for 1970/1971.

18. List of Office Duties for 1970/1971.

19. Pages 122, 125, 126, 127, 134, 139, 140 and 141 of the Non-Descript Daily Book (Exhibit HN/1 No.38).

We are at this stage still taking our Clients' detailed instructions in this matter and, as you can no doubt appreciate, representing three Clients, this takes a great deal of time. We will, however, endeavour to let you know as soon as possible what, if any, witnesses we will require to give oral evidence at the commital proceedings.

Yours faithfully,

KINGSLEY NAPLEY & CO.

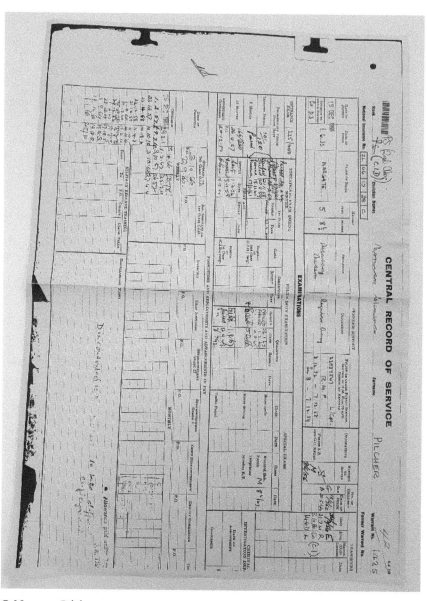

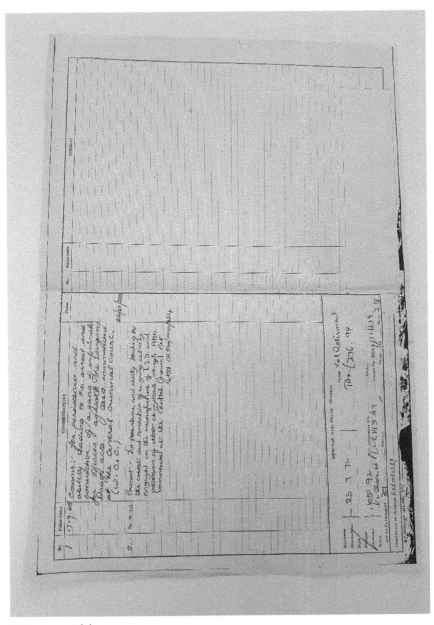

© Norman Pilcher

34 CADOGAN SQUARE
LONDON
SW1X 0JL
01-589 0066

-6. APR 1974

5th April 1974

Dear Nobby,

I had a chat with Mr.Murray of your
solicitors' firm, asking him if it were possible to
have you out on bail, as I could arrange the money
side, but regretfully he said it was not possible.
He did ask me to convery his good wishes to you when
I wrote.

The position is rather complicated until
I can have a conversation with you or your wife contacts
us, but so far we have not heard from her, but I do
feel it would be unfair to you and your wife if I were
to come along on one of the visiting dates. Do rest
assured that we and our friends are concerned with your
plight, and appreciate that you are (as you said) a
victim of politics. From the newspaper reports what
happened stuck out like a sore thumb. I personally do
not believe in the word 'can't' and will do all I can
to reverse what now stands.

Life today is pretty frustrating outside,
and the standard of employees is pathetic. I don't
know where the country's money on education goes,
because in banks and insurance companies where one would
expect to find a bit of intelligence one is faced with
cretans. The mistakes they make are unbelievable. You
or I would not get away with such inefficiency.

You must forgive the outburst. At the moment
my new glasses, which came back with wrong lenses, have
had to go back to the factory and I am permanently living
with dark glasses on - fine out in the sunshine, but

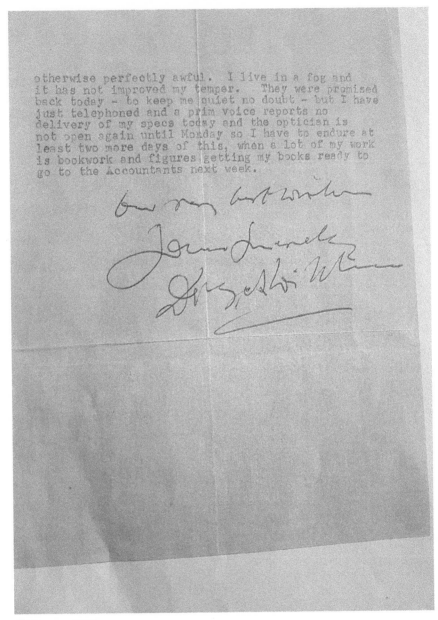

otherwise perfectly awful. I live in a fog and
it has not improved my temper. They were promised
back today - to keep me quiet no doubt - but I have
just telephoned and a prim voice reports no
delivery of my specs today and the optician is
not open again until Monday so I have to endure at
least two more days of this, when a lot of my work
is bookwork and figures getting my books ready to
go to the Accountants next week.

Wally Virgo.

I recall that in late 1970 I was called into Virgo"s office, I wondered what has happened now?. He told me that I had been given a Commissions commendation and commended at the Central Criminal Court. He said "You have done well since you came here this is yet another comm from on high, well done". I replied " Thank but it is a team effort".

Virgo replied " Well you do have a good team with you, we must try to hang on to them, but I will tell that I have suggested that Prichard be promoted".

He seemed to want talk and went on to say" You have to think about your own situation". I said "Promotion for me would mean my transfer out of drugs" Virgo said "Well I could certainly sort that out for you" He continued to say that it would help my cause if I became a freemason and that I could either join a lodge in London or nearer to where I lived. My reply was "I realise that being a mason does help as I have been approached before but I do have my doubts". Virgo replied, "Think about it seriously because it will make a difference to your chances".

Virgo then went on to say " I have been seen by Chief Inspector Kelaher who told me about the problems you are having with information being leaked from your office and I remember that you told me about this before" I replied "Well that is right it is making our job very difficult".

Virgo said that Kelaler had suggested that my team do not show in their diaries and day books their true movements. I said "That's right that will give a chance to get results". Virgo"s reply was "Well I know your problem because it happens all the time, you just do what you have to and keep the results coming in" I thanked him for his advice and left his office later informing the team of the meeting.

It should be remembered that Virgo later denied in court that he had given authority to me to take the action agreed to above. But knowing in retrospect the mindset of the man, one of complete self interest, it came as no surprise that he was willing to lie in court to protect his position.

I hope the reader will have noticed that whilst writing these stories I have made reference to the cultures followed by public services in the UK. These vary slightly within the different areas of service, but I believe that there is a thread running through these cultures. That is where mistakes are made, and we all make mistakes in life, the immediate reaction is a closing of ranks and false statements being made instead of which a ready admission that a mistake was made and that action was being taken to rectify that mistake. The policy always leads to trouble for those concerned. This is common in such areas as the civil service and their masters, politicians, who will who will never admit to making a mistake. I would call this a grey area , but also to be considered is the black area which involves in main our law enforcement bodies.

As I progressed in my early years in the CID I soon realised that the famous scales of justice are heavily weighed in favour of the accused in that the legal system permits those facing trial to lie continually, closely supported by defence counsel who will use any mean to discredit prosecution witnesses who are in the main only seeking justice.
In order to counteract this situation can it be any wonder that investigating officers will take actions, which may be regarded as questionable in order to ensure that those who are obviously guilty of allegations put to them are dealt with by the courts. Unfortunately it must be said that some officers, especially if they are to lazy carry to out a proper investigation blatantly lie and use other acts for various reasons, to ensure convictions.
In my own case regarding our trial we knew that the evidence tendered against us could only have been concocted because it was the reverse of which we knew to be true. Th evidence given by Wally Virgo could at best be said to be evasive but in truth was a pack of lies which later caught up

with him when he appeared in court facing charges of the most serious nature of corruption ever heard at the Old Bailey.

The bottom line is that the legal system together with the culture in the enforcement agencies is clearly not suitable for purpose in the 21st Century. Someone has to grasp the nettle to ensure that institutions look at themselves and realise that action must be taken to rebuild the confidence of the public. A first step, I believe , would be the scrapping of the age old County policing system which should be buried in the past. It would then be a no brainer to form a forward looking National Police Service for England and Wales which could be properly funded and supervised

.

© Norman Pilcher

Chapter 9
Vic Kelaher

Victor Kelaher was born in London where his father served as a detective superintendent. He died when Vic was young and so Vic became a police orphan. It was during this period that he met Wilf Pickles who was also an orphan, and a friendship that was to last over many years began. Vic and Wilf were close which helped Vic, because he was always apprised of information from the intercepts which he could act upon.

Vic served his period of National Service in the RAF Police with the rank of Corporal from 1948 until 1950, mainly in London. He then joined the Met Police rising through the ranks quickly in the C.I.D. He worked in specialist departments including COC8 (the Flying Squad) until 1968 when he was posted to COC1 in the Drugs Squad as Detective Chief Inspector supervising the Squad. I knew of Vic's reputation, which was that of being a very effective and well-informed investigator. It became apparent very quickly that he was well schooled on matters relating to drug abuse and that he was in many ways reclusive. As mentioned, he played his cards close to his chest as a man, but a little too close, long term. The long-term negative consequences of his introversion was his own fear of being caught out. Like a grown up infant, he began to scheme and strategize in a long-term effort to self-protect and avoid being caught in the act. Perhaps if he had been raised in a less troubled way, he would not have behaved with such paranoid habits. Naturally, as he began to see results, benefiting privately from dodgy deals, time seemed to verify to him that his own private process was somehow ethical. Naturally, pride and arrogance tends to display itself and become a kind of shield – but pride comes before a fall.

The information he gathered was in fact very reliable and although the Squad was split into two units, Vic mainly used our unit to carry out enquiries. As a result of the information obtained by him, a number of arrests were made recovering considerable quantities of restricted drugs, which was mainly cannabis resin. As far as we were concerned, we were all batting for the same side and Kelaher was one of us.

Regarding the informants known to Vic, he kept those to himself too, although I did on rare occasions come into contact with a few. During 1969 and 1970 Kelaher became very close to agents from the Bureau of Narcotics and Dangerous Drugs (BNDD) who had a section working in London. I knew that he was still in close contact with Detective Inspector Wilf Pickles who controlled the telephone intercept department situated next to Chelsea Bridge. The association with the BNDD meant that our team was called upon to carry out enquiries on their behalf and although we were making use of intercepts in our enquiries, Vic was also laying on lines for the BNDD agents who we became very familiar with.

On one occasion I travelled to Paris with Kelaher to the US Embassy for a meeting with senior agents. I was not privy to the meetings but later learned that Vic had collected a large sum of cash, which I took to be on behalf of New Scotland Yard. The amount was $62,000. I had to pay for my own flight there, and I doubt Kelaher did hand that money over to the Yard. All of this was going on unbeknownst to us silly mugs and quite frankly, we worked as a team very closely and we didn't have time to think about the politics and the corruption and what Kelaher might or might not have been doing. We were busy working, basically. The fact that there was a war going on between the Customs and the Yard didn't affect us because we very rarely came in contact with Customs. We kept our heads down, continued with work and in a naïve way, let corruption play out behind the scenes in our periphery. Yes, I am sure if we looked up during the time, we would have seen it, but we didn't know to look. And as I've said, we were busy grafting with heads down, digging for clues. As the reader may now fathom, it has taken me time to understand all of this, and let it play through in my own mind for I have spent the last few decades like a man in a cinema watching the same film over and over and over. Doing this as an exercise, one begins to eventually understand the story that they were part of completely and totally, and all of the different character motivations and their Machiavellian intentions become crystal clear.

I travelled to Moreton-in-the-Marsh together with Kelaher and he was talking to senior officers on the subject of the misuse of drugs in the UK. It was obvious that he was held in high regard in relation to the subject. I later learned that the 'powers that be' were looking to Kelaher to become the lead in an overall policy to establish a nationwide task force to deal with the ever-increasing problem and the association Vic had with the US enforcement agencies enhanced his chances to head up such a unit.

I built up a fairly close relationship with Kelaher, mostly in respect of the enquiries that we were making, mainly on the information that our team was gathering, in addition to enquiries passed to us by him. As I have previously noted, I felt that he was reticent in discussing other matters in which he was involved, mainly those relating to the US agencies. I therefore decided to steer clear of those matters with him entirely and the work by our team continued with the full support of every one of our senior officers.

In December 1970 Customs and Excise raided a flat in Holland Park searching for stolen jewellery and furs. The flat was occupied by a man named Rosenblatt and a prostitute. Also present was Vic Kelaher. The prostitute was a Mrs Roberts, the ex-wife of Kofi Roberts who Kelaher had dealt with previously and who was sentenced to a term in prison. As a result of the search a quantity of jewellery was seized, with Kelaher later admitting that he had given Mrs Roberts a watch worth £285, which was also found. He stated that he had purchased the watch in Hatton Garden for her, but why?

In February 1971 a shipment of cannabis was intercepted by Customs at Heathrow and a man named Basil Sands was involved in the matter. Sands was also known to Kelaher, who was not aware that Customs were involved at that time. He allegedly told Sands to take the shipment to the Melba House Hotel in Earl's Court, which was owned then by a friend of his. Customs were keeping observation on the hotel in relation to a man named Babet who had booked a double room at the hotel and on the 5th March, Customs officers disguised as BEA delivery personnel dropped off two cases to the hotel. By 6pm, Sands met Kelaher in Earl's Court and then Kelaher went on to the Melba House Hotel. About an hour later Sands sent a taxi to collect the cases (Kelaher was seen to hold the taxi door open for the driver who put the cases inside). Then, the taxi was followed by Customs officers to the Bayswater Hotel where a man named Nicholson and Babet were arrested. This event was seen by Kelaher who then left the area returning later that evening – to the scene of the crime – only to be detained by the Customs officers and held for several hours. He was duly released, of course, having said… *nothing*. Customs later arrested a total of five persons who were subsequently convicted of conspiracy. Sands, as the ringleader, was sentenced to seven years.

During the course of the trial, serious allegations were made against Kelaher by the defence counsel. The main defendant, Basil Sands, stated that his part in the smuggling of cannabis was as an informant for Kelaher but the evidence gathered by Customs would appear to suggest an even more sinister association. It is difficult to understand why Customs appeared to have 'backed off' taking any action against Kelaher on the evidence available but it may have been that the well-known animosity between Customs and New Scotland Yard influenced such action. The presiding judge in this trial, Mr Justice Trapnell, pointed out to the jury that they were not passing judgement on Kelaher's involvement in the affair. Whilst summing up, the judge stated that 'a forthright attack has been made on the character of Chief Inspector Kelaher, but the jury must not let their opinion of the Inspector sway their verdict, even if in private they believe he was in the middle of the smuggling ring. If he is to be judged, let him be judged by another tribunal on some other occasion.' The prosecution, in their summing up, declared that they had no faith in Kelaher's credibility when John (counsel) said frankly: 'The more we thought about Kelaher's statements, the less we came to the conclusion that Mr Kelaher should be believed.'

The result of this affair was that New Scotland Yard had to submit to an enquiry by an outside force regarding the actions of Vic Kelaher and a team of detectives from Lancashire, headed by Assistant Chief Constable Harold Prescott, commenced their enquiries. This enquiry continued for several months, with dossiers being submitted by the Home Office and others, outlining complaints against the Drugs Squad. The enquiry eventually came to the conclusion that there was no evidence to substantiate any complaints.

Kelaher was after all, our boss and so my team worked closely with him, attending to jobs coming in – we'd help out with the observations but none of us knew what was going on at the time with his prideful corrupt habits, dishonesty and deceit. Perhaps we didn't want to know. This, though, was to be our own downfall. Being suspicious of your superiors, and following your gut in this way regarding the men above you was not normal in those days though, it was not part of the culture then; in fact, the term whistle-blower wasn't even invented back then. The idea that the guv was corrupt and that his guv – Wally Virgo – was basically a villain? This was inconceivable to us as we continued with our work. Perhaps we didn't want to believe it was possible.

Were we in denial? Yes, it is very likely so. We were keeping our head in the sand and avoiding the reality – that corruption was real, and that all it needed to continue was for good men to do nothing. Life was about to present us all with its reality that corruption was more than real, it was endemic to the culture and it would do anything to avoid prison – even if that meant sacrificing its own. Honour among influential men, it seemed, was thin and it was hard to come by. Luckily for me, I was part of a solid team who were unmoving in their morals, their understanding of right and wrong, and so if I was going down for something, we were all going down for it together.

Chapter 10
1970

During 1970 it was clear that on several occasions information regarding our activities was being leaked to the media. The press in general were very fair to the Squad in their reporting of our work and what we were doing, most reporting the facts of the various cases in which we dealt; but it only took one bad apple and there was a section of the media intent on exposing our Squad as corrupt. There were efforts to introduce us to informants at times, who would arrange a set-up, trying to frame me and my men. Typically, arrests would be made, and the informant would often request that he be offered/given some of the drugs seized as payment for the information. There was no way that such a suggestion was agreed to by myself or any member of our unit. The filming unit trying to videotape the bribe set-up was normally quickly discovered and the work destroyed. This tactic was common and it tended to disintegrate quickly when confronted. The fact that people were bent on doing this to us, only encouraged us to become better at our work, wiser and to develop our wits. The *World in Action* programme tried to set us up at one stage. They had information which they received from a drug addict who we had paid (allegedly) with some tablets. This was nonsense. They tried to get him to set us up with him giving us information, us going in, doing a job and then paying him with drugs. It became very obvious very quickly what was going on. It didn't work – nothing happened.

'They won't get anywhere, lads. We haven't done any of this,' I'd tell the team over and over, but Nigel, Nick, Morag, Adam – none of them were bothered.

'It's like a circus out there!'

They wanted to have programmes for the television but like we used to say, if they'd have actually come to us and talked to us, we'd have happily taken them out on raids and let them see what went on but they didn't want to. Instead they wanted to 'play' the part of investigator. Perhaps it was something they enjoyed doing, in the same way a child plays a part on a theatre stage, enjoying themselves and feeling exhilarated, but any genuine investigator would always work scientifically and their methods of inspection were not at all thorough, scientific or rigorous; they were making things up for the telly, shows for people to enjoy, but what we were up against was not a game, and it was not a show. We were in the trenches facing the harsh reality of the criminal underworld, the broken lives caused by drugs and the real hard world.

On one occasion we were investigating a particular dealer operating out of Lordship Lane in South London who was the subject of telephone monitoring. The monitoring had identified a police officer who was attached to a specialised squad who warned the suspect that he was under surveillance by our squad and that his phone calls were being intercepted. This of course meant that our enquiry was terminated. It was this kind of thing which was making our work so difficult.

On another occasion, as a result of information I received, I obtained a warrant to search a suite at the Mayfair Hotel occupied by Levi Stubbs, the lead singer of the Four Tops group. I asked Nigel to carry out the search, as I was not available. He arranged for our team, together with Detective Inspector Bill Peck, to carry out the search. The position was that DI Peck had been posted to the Drugs Squad as a supervising officer. The fact was that he had no interest in the Squad, kept himself away from operational work and was disliked by staff at C1. Whether it was true or not, we believed that this DI who had a contact with the press was sending things out to them, and others too. This was the problem we had with leakages and on serious jobs, it became an earnest matter; on some occasions, the press would arrive before we would.

On arrival at the Mayfair Hotel, Nigel identified a number of photographers lurking in cars and realised once again that information had been leaked to the press. The suite occupied by Stubbs was searched and a quantity of cocaine and ammunition was found, resulting in the arrest of Stubbs by Nigel and charges were subsequently made. The result of the obvious leakage to the press led to a furious argument in the squad between Kelaher, Peck and myself, which resulted in Peck being taken off operational work entirely.

As far as I and the rest of the Squad were concerned it was clear that someone within the department was responsible for the leaking of information. I discussed the situation with Jim Barnett, who also expressed concern and he suggested we keep our movements close to our chests and that I should take such action as was necessary to close down the leaks. I discussed the situation with Kelaher and suggested that, in view of the large cases currently in hand, we should avoid entering our actual movements in the record books. Kelaher considered the matter over and agreed to our not entering our actions into the books and I instructed our team to avoid entering our precise movements in both the Day Book and their diaries whilst the current very difficult state of affairs prevailed. Against this backdrop of key intelligence being leaked, we assumed a rather vigilant position and we chose to enter into a dialogue with Wally Virgo, whose villainous deeds we were still ignorant of. We wanted to make him aware of our thinking, the context of the situation and our actions. It seemed the right thing to do, and checking this across stations also felt right. He seemed to admire how we were demonstrating right process by checking with him. His reply was as a result, simple enough:

'Do what you have to,' he told us, as if he understood fully how we were positioned – between a rock and a hard place.

As a team we therefore made sure that we made entries in the office Day Book and our diaries, which gave no indication of our precise movements. Blocking the leak and healing the wound was paramount during this pressing and sensitive time. Now we knew there was a mole among the ranks, it felt right to arrange an official whisper, at the same table, in the same café in the back corner.

That's the thing: when you are, in police parlance, thief-takers, then you come to peoples' notice. They want to know what you're doing. So we would never discuss anything in the office. We used to sit at the back table of the café and we would talk quietly amongst ourselves about what we were going to do. And that's why we got called the Whispering Squad.

As far as we were concerned, the overriding issue in relation to our evidence-gathering was that our pocket books recorded what we *actually* saw and heard, with absolute accuracy. Everything was above board, everything was transparent in every entry which we all made into our pocket books; these were the only accurate records we kept relating to events. Notes were made at the time or recorded as soon after as was practicable. Anything recorded in other books such as Day Books or diaries was completely irrelevant and not subject to the same standards – and our Squad guvnor knew that. Indeed, any suggestion that such notes were a true record of an officer's movements was, quite frankly, laughable. This was open knowledge within the Squad, a situation forced upon us by the endless corrupt leaks of our movements to both press and criminals.

*

In early 1970 I received a call from a reliable informant who asked that we meet as soon as possible. For the sake of clarity, I will call this man 'Simon'. He had provided me with information resulting in the arrest of a number of what we call 'middle range' dealers. I met Simon at our usual spot at a coffee bar in Charing Cross Station where I found him to be quite agitated and eager to pass on some key information at once. This related to a Middle East national who had offered him ten weights of resin, which he had arranged to collect that evening. The address for the collection was in Kensington with a meeting time of 8pm. I agreed to cover the meeting and gave Simon our funny bankroll for him to use – this consisted of plain paper with an outer cover of real bank notes. I returned to our office, and could see that the team already had a number of warrants to execute that day so I spoke to Nigel, who agreed that we could deal with this case. The drawback was that Simon warned me that the dealer was known to do business whilst armed. It was too late for me to obtain a search warrant so we would have to deal with things as they arose. Nigel and I left the office at about 6.30pm and I was carrying my own revolver. I was familiar with that gun, and practised weekly.

My arrangements with Simon were that we would cover his entry to the premises and give him ten minutes before we entered. At about 8.10pm Simon arrived and entered the house, which had been answered by a man. The front ground floor light went on so we had a good idea where they were. We waited about fifteen minutes then gained entry through the front using my trusty keys. The door to the front room was ajar and we could clearly hear a conversation, which was to say the least, very heated. Nigel checked the rear room, which had a door leading to the front room. We agreed that Nigel cover the rear whilst I'd move into the front room. As the result of Simon's heads-up that the dealer might be armed, I drew my firearm and quietly entered. What I saw was not good: Simon was there seated on a chair with the dealer holding a pistol to his head.

'Blimey,' I said to myself.

The fact was, that this would go very wrong if not dealt with cautiously. Because I had been trained with firearms I knew to keep a very cool head, so I kept the 'I'm in the shit here' to myself. Nigel moved in from the back room, so we had a stand-off situation. I told the suspect that we were police officers and to put his weapon down. He seemed to be very calm and said that he would shoot Simon, who was trying to rip him off. A conversation ensued back and forth between myself and the suspect but I was determined to stand by Churchill's statement, 'Jaw Jaw, not War War' and so I made it clear to the suspect that if he used his weapon, I would not hesitate to take him out.

Then Nigel said to the suspect, 'You really need to think about what you're doing. We've been in these situations before and I suspect you haven't. You're in what we call the seven-yard range. So one of the things that's going to happen here, is that Nobby isn't going to miss. The next thing is, that he's going to fire two bullets before you've even moved your finger on the trigger. And those two are going to go straight in your chest. It's going to blow you backwards and the next thing that's going to happen is that we're going to be trying to save your life. Your blood will be pumping out all over the shop. So what I'm suggesting to you is that you drop the gun, very gently, and not be bloody stupid, otherwise you're going to be dead. I've seen this happen before – we've done this before. Just don't be silly.'

You have to be very clear and very determined when you're in that situation. There were no two more determined in that room than Nigel and me, because number one, he's not shooting and number two, the only way out of this is he either drops the gun or he dies.

Whilst talking I had a good opportunity to study the weapon he was holding and I believed it may well have been a replica gun, but I could not be positive so had to act on the premise that it was genuine. I told the suspect that if this incident went no further he was at worst facing a few years in prison because any mention of the firearm simply would not happen.

'So you have two options to choose from,' I told him. 'ONE – if I think you are going to use the weapon, I will have no choice but to shoot. TWO – if you hand the weapon over you will only be charged for possession.' He understood what I meant: if he handed over the weapon and any cannabis in his possession, he would only face charges relating to the drugs.

I could see that he was thinking over my suggestions but it was clear that he wanted to deal with Simon who he thought had double-crossed him and had brought us into the deal. I told him that I did not know Simon and that he should be more careful when using the telephone. He seemed to take on board how we had become involved and after a conversation with Nigel, who persuaded him to listen to the offer put to him, he handed over the weapon to Nigel after a period of thought. Nigel, who knew more about weapons than most, realised straight away that the weapon was a very good replica – a fact that suited the situation.

We recovered ten weights of resin and charged the man with possession with intent to supply. The replica gun I broke down and dumped; Simon was looked after financially and he continued to supply me with information.

In retrospect I have often asked myself: would I have taken the action required had the matter gone the wrong way? Would I have shot the man down? Yes, I would have. I would have shot him dead.

The end result of this matter was that we were able to prevent a large amount of drugs hitting the streets. The suspect pleaded guilty and was sentenced to three years imprisonment. It was good work, and it marked a step-change for us.

1970 was the important year because following this event, we decided to stop the possession charges and rely on the supply charges solely. Loose ends were tied up, there were no small possession charges we needed to chase down, and that meant jumping back on the Salah lead. I picked up the phone and made contact with my greatest informant – The Man With No Name.

Chapter 11
The Salah Saga

After the arrest of Wilkins and with the amount of cannabis resin in his possession, I realised that the information given to me by him meant I would have to discuss the situation as a whole with the guvnor, Vic Kelaher. At that stage it would appear that the Salah family had recently imported 900lbs of top grade resin into the UK, most of which had been put into circulation.

I looked into the make-up of the Salah family. They came from Birmingham and were part of the old cotton trade. They were Pakistani retailers, selling what people wanted, ultimately. They came down to London where they saw opportunity to import and export but not cotton – drugs. They were: Father – Mohammed Salah; Mother – Kathleen Salah; Son – John Salah; Daughters – Janet Salah and Kathy Salah.

John Salah had one conviction for possession of cannabis but there was nothing recorded against the rest of the family. Before discussing the matter with Kelaher, I wanted to make enquiries regarding the family, so I arranged a meeting with a man I regarded as being the best-informed person I knew regarding 'activities' in London. The man concerned, who I knew only as 'The Man With No Name'. He was a highly successful cat burglar who resided at a top-of-the-range property off Eaton Square. He had been involved in criminal activities for over forty years, operating at all times on his own and never having been arrested, mixing with the so-called upper crust of society. I had not been in place in the Drugs Squad for very long when I received a call at Old Scotland Yard from him requesting a meeting. I obviously agreed and we had our first meeting in the Sherlock Holmes public house off Northumberland Avenue. There, after exchanging the usual pleasantries, he explained that he had a keen interest in the drugs problem in the UK. With his connections in the criminal world he was constantly being offered deals relating to drugs distribution. He had become involved because of his own personal mission. He hated drug dealers. So much so, that he would do anything to help bring them down. Early on, he made it clear that he did not want to be regarded as a so-called informant but that he was willing to assist me if he could. He had in fact been referred to me by a senior C.I.D. officer with whom he was acquainted. He was a modern day Robin Hood, a cat burglar and he hated drug dealers passionately. He had never been arrested, knew every person at Scotland Yard, but nobody had any idea what he did or who he was, but the one thing he did… help take out the drug dealers. He absolutely hated them. He was a gentleman and he always worked alone. 'The secret is to work alone,' he'd say, 'and you don't have to rely on other people to keep their mouths shut.' He was in his 50s when I met him, and he was – a nicer chap you couldn't meet, never hurting anybody, apart from the insurance companies. Quite frankly I could not believe how passionately he hated drug dealers, maybe he had a daughter once who died from drugs. I could only presume, for I never asked him why.

When we met, I took the opportunity to ask him if he had any knowledge regarding the Salah family. He thought for some time and then spoke as if choosing to select his response wisely. It was as if I was sat opposite Cary Grant in *To Catch A Thief*. He said that he had heard that a Pakistani family had brought in a 'considerable quantity' of resin very recently, which was being moved around London. He then paused and warned me to be 'careful' as the family had a contact in the service. His head lowered and I waited for him. It was clear that he was ready to say something else, and I waited for it. 'I'll try and help Nobby, but do be careful. Truly.' His head lifted and he stared into my eyes. He stood up and left the Sherlock Holmes pub. He was The Man With No Name and it was the last time I saw him.

I regarded this meeting as confirmation that we should commence enquiries into the Salah's and I later discussed the information I had with Kelaher who agreed that our unit should make this enquiry a priority. He later spoke to Wilf Pickles, the officer in charge of the telephone monitoring unit, who made it clear that at that time the necessary lines were not available. As a result of this, although I was keen not to do it, I asked Customs if they had any spare lines. I was not surprised to receive a knockback for this request.

At the beginning of October 1970 it was decided that our unit would commit full time to investigating the Salah family. It therefore fell upon me to ensure that the enquiry would be carried out thoroughly. The rest of the team were DC Nick Prichard, DC Nigel Lilley, DC Adam Acworth, DC Morag McGibbon and DI Joe Bolton who had recently joined the Drugs Squad. We as a team had been working together for some time now and I knew that I could not have wished for a better unit to carry out diligently what would be a long and complex enquiry.

The Salah's were at this time residing at The Meads, Stoke Poges, where, from the 27th October their telephone was monitored until the beginning of November when Mr and Mrs Mohammed Salah moved house to Kier Park House, Ascot; this being a very substantial property situated close to Ascot Racecourse. John and Kathy Salah moved to 29 Mapledene Road, Langley, where the telephone was also monitored, recording calls made by Mrs Salah to John. These calls indicated that moves were being made to import a further quantity of drugs into the country. At this time evidence obtained through the monitoring system was not admissible in court but those initial conversations were as follows:

Mum:	Hello, John.
John:	All right, Mum?
Mum:	Yes. Ni-Ar's [sounds like] had his letter.
John:	Yeah.
Mum:	He said if you want the pants and vests [emphasised] you must give an order for two and a half months before.
John:	Yeah.
Mum:	He said it's very bad in Afghanistan now for white people.
John:	Yeah.
Mum:	Well – I don't want to go, John. I think it would be better if your father went.
John:	Yeah.
Mum:	He said that there are customers for the pants all the time, and that much of the stuff that is sold is of very inferior quality.
John:	Yeah.
Mum:	You know – so he said if we want to order these vests, I have to put down fifty per cent first.
John:	Yeah. That's all right.
Mum:	I've been today about the van. It still hasn't come.
John:	It's due though, isn't it?
Mum:	It's due – but it hasn't come in.
John:	Shouldn't talk on the phone, Mum, really. Right. I'll come round tomorrow afternoon and we'll have a chat about it…

They then had a general conversation about the dog having a rash. The words in brackets were the telephone-typist's comments. Ni-Ar's was in fact Niaz Ali, a relation of Mohammed. Two hours later Mum was on the phone again.

Mum:	John, I've just read this letter again, and what they want is fifty per cent deposit and also the price is up fifty per cent.
John:	Oh.
Mum:	Where I had the letter from he said that there is other people who grow it specially – you know, the wool.
John:	Yeah.
Mum:	Like – it's fleecy-lined.
John:	So it's gone up.
Mum:	They said half as much again.
John:	That's no good, Mum.
Mum:	Yeah. Your father's a bit upset about it.
John:	That's been cooked.
Mum:	Looks like it.
John:	To put us off.
Mum:	No. Not to put us off. To get a cut.
John:	A cut for [sounds like] Ni-Ar-Zally [phonetic]. Or he's wrote to the old man. Or the old man's wrote to him behind our back to tell him to write that letter.
Mum:	No, he hasn't. That's nonsense.
John:	Is it?
Mum:	Yes.
John:	Well, you'd better write back then, and tell them that it's got to be at the old price or to forget it.
Mum:	Yes, we'll sort something out.
John:	If it's a little bit more, it doesn't matter.
Mum:	It does matter. The price will have to go up anyhow.
John:	Yeah.
Mum:	That's why it's costing more. Because the price has gone up. They just took us for a ride, you know, with the last lot.
John:	Yeah…

A few minutes later John telephoned his mother, and advised her:

John: Play along with the old man. If Dad goes out there, he'll come to some arrangement with them anyhow.

To which Mum replied:

Mum: Yeah. I can't afford to cross him.

As can be seen, reference is made to pants and vests in the conversations. I was satisfied that these conversations were suggesting that the family intended doing business with the source as with their previous transactions. As a result of these and many other conversations it was important that we carried out long periods of observation to obtain the evidence required for any prosecutions.

During the following weeks, constant observations were kept on the family at the addresses in an effort to identify any associates. Numerous telephone conversations were recorded which confirmed that a visit to Pakistan was imminent on Tuesday 15th December 1970. We kept observations on the premises of Wilsons, motor traders in Kings Avenue, Brixton. Mohammed and John Salah and another man were seen in the offices and then seen looking at a Land Rover vehicle, leaving later in a Mini driven by the unknown man.

On 16th December observation was again being kept on the Brixton address by Detective Inspector Bolton, Nigel and Adam where they saw the Land Rover, index number EMG456J. They also noted the presence of a Volkswagen, index number RPP24H, together with Mrs Kathleen Salah, John and Janet Salah. After a short period, John was seen to drive off in the Land Rover followed by Kathleen and Janet in the Volkswagen. Observations were kept on Kier Park House until the early hours on that night but there was no further sighting of the Land Rover. The vehicle was not seen again until the 21st December outside Kier Park House. This was a quiet period but observations were kept on the family's movements. It was known from telephone conversations that Mohammed was planning to fly to Pakistan to finalise the purchase of the cannabis. After a number of delays he flew out of Heathrow on the 5th January 1971.

On the 4th January John phoned his sister Janet for a chat about a trailer under construction at Crevald's Boatyard. The following conversation was recorded:

John:	I've just spoken to the builders, and he said the interior depth will be just over three feet. It won't be enough, Janet.
Janet:	It won't be enough.
John:	We will have to make it bigger. It's eleven feet long and five feet wide. I said I'll be in in the morning.
Janet:	Well, if we make it higher and put a mirror in, it will look as though we are using it for our clothing and camping equipment.
John:	I'll pop round and we can finalize it for tomorrow morning.
Janet:	Yes. Okay then.
John:	And can you come with me? Only I'm taking the Land Rover with me. About nine.
Janet:	I don't know.
John:	Well, look – you must soon make your mind up because he only has ten or twelve days to do it.
Janet:	Well, I've got to see about the flight. Well, look – we'll scrap the boat idea, and have it done nice inside.
John:	Yes. Okay – I know what we want.

The trailer concerned was not in fact collected until the following week, all of these activities being observed by our team. On the 7th January as a result of the enquiries that I had made, I located the Highwayman van, index number PBH24H, in Chadwell Heath and together with Morag I examined the vehicle, which had been fitted with a false floor. The vehicle was thoroughly examined and photographed for evidential purposes and on the 12th January John phoned Kathleen and told her that the trailer would be ready on the 14th. Then on the 13th January Kathleen was heard to have the following conversation with John:

Mum:	Hallo, John. I've got the flu now.
John:	Have you?
Mum:	I just want to ask you a very simple question.
John:	What?
Mum:	You know if you've got four library books and you put them on top of each other and you measure them – but on the other hand, if you put two one side and two on top of one another you're not taking up so much space, are you?

John:	You are – because it doesn't matter. Because they are still equal amounts.
Mum:	But I've just measured them, and they are ten inches high. And if you take the other two the other way – you see what I mean – you cut it down to five inches high.
John:	You haven't – because you're still taking up the same area width-wise. So therefore it doesn't make any difference. You can't put a pint of milk into a half-pint jug.
Mum:	No. But you can stack a thing away, so that –
John:	Yeah. I know what you mean. And that's the way I'm doing it, Mum.

Observations were kept at the boatyard when the Land Rover arrived at about 9.45am with John and Janet in it. They both entered the offices where they stayed until 11am. Adam managed to take a number of photographs of the trailer and on the 17th January, together with Detective Chief Inspector Kelaher, we kept observation on Kier Park House from 10.20am to 10.00pm. During that period we saw the trailer in front of the garage. We saw John, Janet and their mother apparently working on it and Janet left Kier Park House in the Land Rover at about 9.30pm.

Apart from this case we were involved in other work matters, at various times being called upon to assist other squads with enquiries. It was a busy period and considering the leak in-house, it was also important that details regarding the Salah's be kept quiet to avoid what came to be known as 'the big problem': a mole leaking intelligence out. As a result of this I had no problem with each member of our team maintaining meticulous notes of all our observations of the Salah's activities, as I was the one who signed off their notes in their pocket books. At this stage it was clear that the evidence already gathered was leading to the successful convictions of the Salah's and the likelihood of our removing a large quantity of cannabis from the streets.

It was known that the Salah's held a bank account at Coutts Bank in Jersey. On the 24th January, Janet was seen catching a flight to Jersey probably to draw out cash to finance their current venture. In the middle of January (about the 22nd) a letter was sent from Mohammed, who was still in Lahore, to John which read as follows:

Dear John,

I am sorry to say I am not wrote your letter soon when I reached Pakistan. John I have been to Pershore 9th January and came back 10th January night about 8.30 p.m. 13th January I was taken ill. I had very bad flu & temperature. Since 13th Jan. I never get of the bed and I don't know what is going on. So Doctor came to see me he spend about 1 hour to examine me. So I start treatment. Take me seven to eight days to get better. So I feel real weak. Please tell Jan & your mother DO NOT start 31 Jan. & 1 February. I have cancelled everything. We will start fresh again. DON'T start till you hear from me. I find out everything. Why should we pay NR (New Rupees) 9 1/2 thousand Deposit to get the goods. They want to put their profit fist away and to start make goods. So I said NO. Don't worry I will get my own terms on time. When the time is come. It will come soon. I am not coming back till I find proper place and right price. Wish you understand my point. Don't worry. Thing will turn better. I feel the KHAN is very big dog now. Please let know has he growing. Anyhow remember me to Khan and Kathy. How is Kathy? Is she still under the Doctor? And look after your health.

Give my love to Kathy & to you & Jan & your mother.

Love from Dad.

Unfortunately for the family this letter did not arrive until late March due to a postal strike. The family therefore carried on with their arrangements unaware of the situation in Lahore.

On the 31st January 1971 John left in the Land Rover and trailer to travel to Lahore. Adam and I maintained observations in Slough and Ascot, later driving down to Dover to resume our observation at the ferry terminal. At 10.30pm we identified the Land Rover entering the port. The trailer was attached to the Land Rover which was occupied by John, Kathleen and Janet. Adam and I watched as the family checked in through departure, eventually boarding the ferry at 12.30am, which subsequently left for Ostend. I waved them a fond farewell in the knowledge that, with luck, we would meet again in about two months. I felt quite relieved that we could now have a rest from continued travelling and long periods of observations and spend some time with what I liked to call the bread and butter cases.

On my return to the office I gathered our team together, with the exception of Adam who had gone away on a well-earned leave. I spent some time checking the pocket books of all concerned, which as I expected were spot on in view of the length of this enquiry. I was not concerned with our diaries as we and our supervising officers were well aware that those records were kept fictitious, the internal mole never being far from our thoughts. In the meantime, John had returned home with his father on the 26th February leaving Kathleen and Janet to drive from Pakistan with the goods. We tracked the women across Asia Minor through bad weather and on the 28th February John telephoned a doctor as follows:

Doctor:	Hallo. How did you get on?
John:	Terrible.
Doctor:	Did you get there all right?
John:	Yes. But the Land Rover is busted up. We picked the worst time of the year.
Doctor:	What? – the Land Rover isn't fit to come back?
John:	It's been through quite a bit. I was in the middle of nowhere, trying to flag down three flaming Arabs as I went off the road. Nobody would stop. My feet and hands started to freeze, it was so cold. And all the gas froze up inside the Land Rover. About five minutes later, six Land Rovers came round the bend – all full of American students. They had all the winching equipment and they got me out in ten minutes. Otherwise we would have frozen to death.
Doctor:	How long did it take you to get there?
John:	Two weeks. They wouldn't let us in. Then there was some trouble at the borders. Apart from that, two chaps have been killed.
Doctor:	What? Out there?
John:	Yes.
Doctor:	Oh, crumbs.
John:	I'll have to explain when I see you.

Then followed a general conversation about John's ailments, which included stomach trouble and the fact that he had strained his back passage. John seemed to be after some buckshee medical advice. But the doctor was still curious about the trip.

Doctor:	When did they leave?
John:	Monday.
Doctor:	You stayed on for a few days, did you?
John:	Yes – but we have had a lot of trouble, a lot of trouble.
Doctor:	How is the car now?
John:	It's going to be all right. It's been off the road a few times. We've had a lot of trouble amongst ourselves. I'm worried to death, as two people were killed with the consignment. I'll have to explain to you when I see you.
Doctor:	But the consignment you've got.
John:	Only half of what we want because a lorry was hi-jacked and they were shot dead.
Doctor:	Is it enough to make it worthwhile? That's the thing.
John:	Just about, I think. But you know, it's a lot of trouble.
Doctor:	So you didn't need the trailer really.
John:	No. As it turned out, we didn't. I'll tell you when I see you. I don't want to talk on the phone, you know.
Doctor:	Well, if you hear anything, let me know.
John:	I don't think I will. I tried to send a telex to my wife and did everything possible to get a message in, but it's just hopeless. I paid somebody £5 to send a telex, and they said that she would get it. Of course I arrived yesterday and she hadn't heard anything. She has been worried to death.
Doctor:	So really they left on Monday – which means if they are going along well, they should be approaching Turkey by now.
John:	Yes. But Janet said to me if the conditions are that bad, she's going to stop and wait until it gets better. It's so dangerous out there. She's only a girl you know. The driving – I've never seen nothing like it in my life. Anyhow, I'll tell you all about it on Friday.

Although we never involved this doctor in our enquiries, I leave it up to the reader to make up their mind as to whether or not the doctor was aware of the Salah's activities.

As a result of three members of the family now being abroad, I cut back on our observations but we still maintained a casual system because of our backlog of other cases. A message was received on the 9th March from 'Mason' – a pseudonym for the Salah's. Kathy took the call from Bulgaria which read 'Delayed Bulgaria until end of month – Mum.'

When I saw this message I must admit that I thought we were going to have problems. It appeared that the women were delayed on the Bulgarian border. On Friday 19th March a man called Sid phoned John who explained how concerned he was for the welfare of Kathleen and Janet. About a week later John was at home with Kathy when the phone rang at 5.30pm.

Man:	Is that John Mason?
John:	Speaking.
Man:	You don't know me – but I've just hitch-hiked through Bulgaria, and I've got a message from your mother.
John:	Yes?
Man:	She has been detained in Bulgaria by the authorities.
John:	Yes.
Man:	Janet is in jail
John:	In jail!
Man:	Yes. Apparently there was some dispute with an American about the trailer, I believe, and the police got to know. Anyway, I think your mother tried to bribe them, and they confiscated the car and the trailer. Your mother is under arrest, but she's in a hotel. Janet is in prison, and they're trying to make her confess. Do you understand?
John:	Yes. Yes. Oh, dear. Do you know where they are?
Man:	No, I'm afraid I've forgotten the name of the town. But it's on the border somewhere.
John:	All right. Thank you.
Man:	That's all I can tell you. Apparently your mother can't write, or anything like that.
John:	Okay. Thank you.

This conversation was a little short of being disastrous for the family. As for ourselves, we were disappointed after hundreds of hours of work, but it was still likely that we would be preventing large quantities of drugs reaching our streets. It would appear that Janet was detained in prison whilst Kathleen was in a hotel. There was another call from 'Sid':

Sid:	Did you want to speak to me?
John:	Yes, they've been done.
Sid:	For certain?
John:	Yes, for certain. A hitchhiker told me. In Bulgaria. Apparently they've got Janet in jail. I'll have to go out there, Sid – care to come? I could use some help now.
Sid:	When are you thinking of going?.
John:	Monday, I think I'll go by car. It'll take about three days.
Sid:	I'll come down tomorrow afternoon, John.
John:	I'll be very grateful. I don't even know the town, it's really serious.
Sid:	Okay. I'll come tomorrow about one.

It would appear that John intended travelling to Bulgaria and was trying to contact the hitchhiker who had informed him of the arrest of the women. It was clear to me that we now had to make our move against the family so I obtained search warrants for both addresses occupied by the family. The team then made plans to bring the case to a close.

It was Saturday 20th March 1971, nine months since the start of the enquiries, and I sent Nigel and Adam out to Ascot and Slough to check the situation. Together with Morag and Adam I went to 29 Mapledene Road where at 12 noon we entered the house. There in the house were John, Mohammed and Kathy, John's wife. I told them that we were going to execute a search warrant for drugs and that we were making enquiries regarding the arrest of Kathleen and Janet found in possession of cannabis resin. John admitted that they had received a phone call regarding the arrest but claimed that it was a frame-up and asked, 'Can I do anything for you?' I obviously realised what he was getting around to but I still asked what he meant. He suggested that his mother would sort it out. My response was that if he was 'suggesting what I thought' then he had better 'say no more' or he would find himself in 'deeper shit'. John's response was to say, 'Never mind! Someone will take it.' They were then told that observations had been kept on their activities in purchasing the Land Rover and their alterations to the trailer. John denied any involvement.

As a result of the search, various documents were found relating to the alterations to the trailer and the issue of travel documents to Afghanistan. Based on these discoveries I arrested all three and they were cautioned. I was the one who interviewed them all, and the details of those interviews were the subject of Nick's evidence given during the later trial. John, Mohammed and Kathy were taken to Cannon Row Police Station where the relevant paperwork was completed. They were charged with conspiracy to import cannabis into the UK and their appearance at Bow Street Magistrates Court resulted in John and Mohammed being remanded in custody while Kathy was granted bail.

In view of the activities in Bulgaria it was imperative that evidence be obtained to support the case in the UK. Detective Inspector Joe Bolton and I travelled to Sofia, Bulgaria where after discussions with the Bulgarian authorities we interviewed Janet on the 2nd April in Sofia Central Prison. She had been sentenced to a term in the prison. On the 3rd of April we interviewed Mrs Salah in the British Embassy in Sofia. We also examined the Land Rover and trailer confirming that these were the vehicles seen in the UK. The trailer contained, in my estimation, 616 packets of resin and we took possession of one packet for evidential purposes and took photographs of the vehicles. The cannabis was later sent through the Embassy bag to the UK where I took possession of it on my return.

As a result of a request from the Bulgarian authorities, Joe and I agreed to attend a press conference regarding the Salah family. The whole thing turned out to be completely shambolic. It had been set up to emphasise how corrupt Western society was and how ridden it was with drug dependents and criminals. Joe decided to walk out and we returned to the UK having achieved our objective of obtaining evidence.

On my return to the office, the paperwork had to be completed for the prosecution. During the course of the enquiry about 500 conversations had been recorded by CII for which we were truly grateful. Although these intercepts could not be used in court, the evidence that we had gathered made up a watertight case against the Salah's. During the post-arrest period, both Kathleen and Janet remained in Bulgaria – Janet in custody and Kathleen, for some reason, on bail. It soon became clear why Kathleen was free as she returned to the UK where she withdrew £90,000 from their account, then returned to Bulgaria and paid over the cash whereupon Janet was released from prison. When I received this information, I obtained warrants for their arrest when they returned to the UK.

*

The trial of the Salah's – Mohammed, John and Kathy – began at the Old Bailey on the 7th September 1971. The presiding judge was Mr Justice Gillis QC and the prosecution was led by Mr Corkery QC who outlined the charges being put before the Salah's of conspiracy to import, possess and supply cannabis resin, to which they pleaded not guilty. The prosecution laid out in detail, for the jury, all of the events leading up to their arrests including the evidence of our team. The defence was conducted by Mr Hudson QC and Mr Lloyd-Ely QC who obviously denied on behalf of their clients any wrongdoing. The case took the usual route of allegation and denial but it was clear that the defence were in a difficult position. During the questioning of Nick, Mr Lloyd-Ely asked suddenly if he kept any other records of his movements other than his pocket book. Nick stated that he did in fact keep Day Books in the office and a personal diary. During my long period in the service which involved countless appearances in court I had never heard that question asked on any occasion, and I soon realised that should these records be produced that they would of course not tally with our pocket books. At that stage I was not particularly concerned because the action that we had taken had been authorised by our senior officers in an effort to avoid leakages from our office regarding our movements.

There was a third defence counsel, Mr Ronald Shulman, who appeared on behalf of Kathy making a strong defence that she knew nothing of the events. Mr Shulman was named the following year as being involved in the 'Shilling Will' trial in which three men were involved. Two were convicted but Shulman fled the country. In August 1973 his legal peers found him guilty in his absence and expelled him from his Inn of Court.

During the course of the telephone intercepts, conversations had been noted between a doctor and a man simply called Sid. The recordings clearly indicated both were aware of the Salah's actions. We discussed their possible involvement but decided not follow up on this situation as the recordings were not of evidential value but were valuable as information. Had we taken the matter further both the doctor and Sid would have been unresponsive to any questioning. I believed that Sid may well have been the serving police officer who was known to the Salah's and the use of the name Sid could well have indicated that he served in the CID.

As was his duty, Mr Lloyd-Ely made great play on the fact that our pocket books, from which we gave evidence, did not compare with our personal diaries. The conclusion of the trial was reached on the 13th October with the jury retiring to consider their verdicts. The jury returned at 7.45pm and when asked, the foreman announced that Mohammed, John and Kathy had been found guilty. Mohammed was jailed for five years with costs of £2000. John was sentenced to three years with £1500 costs. Kathy, who was heavily pregnant, was sentenced to nine months imprisonment and suspended for three years. All the findings were unanimous, in other words there was no doubt that the family had been involved in drug trafficking. As for the result, I never concerned myself with any action taken by the courts. My job finished when I presented the facts before the court. I walked out and that was the end of it. Or so I thought.

As a result of the Sands trial, mentioned previously, Robert Mark had instituted an enquiry into the conduct of Vic Kelaher. The result of the enquiry was that Kelaher was transferred from the Drugs Squad to administrative work at New Scotland Yard. The enquiry, carried out by an outside force, found that there was insufficient evidence for action to be taken against him but Mark was determined that Kelaher should be dealt with in some way and ordered a further enquiry to be carried out into the allegations made during the Salah trial. Why? Because it was the last case in which Kelaher had been involved. The real Salah saga had only just begun.

Mark set up a team of detectives to carry out the enquiry and he included uniformed Chief Inspector Ernest Faulkner to ensure that he was kept fully aware of the progress in the matter. Faulkner was, as I later discovered, a particularly unpleasant person who was 'in it to win it' or, in other words, to seek further promotion. What would he do for Mark to achieve this promotion? Anything Mark needed. I didn't mind a man playing for keeps, but when he'd go to any length to win a status symbol, I'd normally walk away from such a man because the world validating him was more significant than a strong handshake. They were men who yearned for acceptance. They were not men who knew values, and the value of saying what they meant and meaning what they'd say. They were not men who could be trusted, and you want to be with men who have got your back in this world, especially when busting down doors, not men who tell you what you want to hear. True friends tell you what is difficult to know but the truth is sometimes very difficult to hear.

On the 10th June 1971, notice was given in police orders that I was to be transferred from the Drugs Squad to L Division. With immediate effect, it was the end of my time with the unit. The Whispering Squad was then no more. I had not been informed by my senior officers of the move but had to learn of it by phone from a friend. At the time I thought this all to be in line with the very poor standard of decision-making within New Scotland Yard but I was posted to Clapham police station and I immediately felt at home. The fact was that I was glad to be away from the overbearing toxic atmosphere at New Scotland Yard. The office at Clapham was supervised by an excellent Detective Inspector who was very conscious of the welfare of his staff and went on to achieve the highest ranks within the CID in the following years. I spent a very happy eighteen months on Division but meanwhile, the enquiry Robert Mark was pushing carried on for some time, causing all concerned upsetting periods of being hassled by the enquiry team at his behest.

During my tenure at C1, I had kept notes of my contacts in a notebook which I kept close to myself. This book had a coloured cover. I kept the contact numbers for all of the informants with whom I worked, kept in a coded fashion which I had devised to prevent the information being misused. When I was transferred to Division, the book went with me, together with my current police diary.

This diary was collected from Clapham CID office by a member of the enquiry team in my absence. I later looked for the notebook but could not locate it. I contacted a member of the team asking if they had taken it but they denied any knowledge of it. I later learned that statements had been taken from all the staff in the CID office asking if anybody had seen this book in my possession when only one detective constable stated that he had seen it in my possession.

I came to the conclusion that this book had been removed by the enquiry team together with my diary and kept under wraps because some entries would confirm statements which I had made.

Maybe I should have lodged a complaint that the book had been stolen but I knew that such an action would have been met with a negative response. The fact was that when requested to submit written statements, the staff at Clapham produced statements which were identical in content, with the exception of one statement which confirmed that the book existed. The probability was that the statements had been produced and presented for signature, a common practice used by enquiry staff working within AIO at New Scotland Yard.

Back to Robert Mark. He worked for himself and his beeline mission to become a Lord was beyond question. The consequences of his forceful mission, Kelaher's corruption and the drugs business made for many a dark cloud to settle above me, my family and life in general. Nothing was moving in the right direction, nothing was sunny and joyous and so I chose to confide in those closest to me – Nigel, Nick, Adam and Morag. We met for a catch up in the old Italian café and I told them how I wanted to change my life.

It was during early 1972 that I decided I would begin looking elsewhere to continue my career. I had a number of former colleagues who had moved to Australia for the same reason and I discussed the situation at length with Shirley. We began looking at the pros and cons of such a move. I travelled to Perth in Western Australia where I met a number of friends, looked at the feasibility of joining the enforcement agencies and looked at the property there. I decided that such a move would greatly enhance our family life. Like many Brits, I simply loved Australia. What was happening back in London was too dark and rotten. I did not like the corruption and the non-stop enquiries at the behest of Mark and his private ambitions to clean Kelaher out. To put it bluntly, I wanted a bit of sun in my life.

Following our decision to move, I contacted Wally Virgo at C1 and told him of my decision. At first he questioned what I intended to do, because I still had a good future in London. I asked him if he would check with the enquiry team as to whether it was in order for me to move to Perth. Because I was being investigated, I needed to know that the enquiry team investigating were okay with my leaving.

I soon received a call from Virgo who told me that the enquiry team could see no reason why I should not carry on with my plans and on the 23rd July 1972 I tendered my resignation to leave the service with a real feeling of regret. Although I was looking forward to Australia, I truly treasured every moment I had spent in the Force and I knew that I would miss the friends I had made. I later received a phone call from Superintendent Gordon Mees, the officer leading the internal enquiry into the Salah case. He told me that he had spoken to Virgo about my leaving the country. He said that as far as he was concerned there was no problem but that the enquiry was going to continue. He wished me the best of luck in Australia saying that although he was heading up the enquiry he was not happy with the situation as he was himself up against it – in a position where Mark had inserted a uniform Chief Inspector, Faulkner, into the team, obviously to ensure that he, Mark, was on top of the progress and process of their enquiries. Mees also said he was not happy with the situation that myself and the team had found ourselves in. He said that he had pointed out to Mark at a meeting that Mark's determination to deal with Kelaher was putting five good officers' futures in jeopardy. Apparently Mark's response was that Kelaher must be dealt with and that we were all *collateral damage*. Mees finished the call saying that his position was impossible, advising me not to talk to Faulkner when questioned.

The internal enquiry continued for some months with a view being expressed by Faulkner, whilst interviewing our team, that Nigel, Nick and I had falsely stated that two observations about which we had given evidence had been 'fabricated' because the evidence against the Salahs was insufficient to obtain a conviction. Faulkner also suggested that the evidence had been built up as a result of 'intercept recording'. The truth was that conversations were recorded indicating that meetings had been arranged by the Salahs. Having this information, it would have been a failure in our duty had we not witnessed these meetings. The fact was that these two observations, which were later to be the subject of prosecutions, were of no evidential value during the Salah trial. The observations had been kept as described and noted in our pocket books. As was customary, such notes were included in our statement of evidence. As a result of the ongoing enquiry, the Director of Public Prosecutions (DPP) office suggested to the Salahs' legal team that they should appeal against their convictions, which would not be opposed by the prosecution. During the appeal hearing the prosecution did not oppose the appeal but made it clear that the Salahs had been involved in the offence of which they had been convicted. Mr Hudson QC, appearing for the Salahs at their appeal, said the basis for the appeals was that the jury's verdict was unsafe and unsatisfactory. No criticism, he said, could be made of the conduct of the trial.

The Salahs were released from prison and no further action was taken against Kathleen and Janet Salah. The situation at that stage was this: the Salahs had been released even though the case had resulted in their convictions, notwithstanding the fact that no decision had been made to take action against the officers involved in the case. Should the enquiry have found no case to answer against our team, the DPP's office would have had egg on their face and thus faced severe criticism from the press. As a direct result of this decision, the DPP had to ensure that action must be taken against our team. Let me put it bluntly: my team and I were sacrificed on the altar of political expediency. Someone had to take the blame.

There had been high-level meetings held between the Home Office,

Customs and New Scotland Yard in an effort to settle the difference between Customs and the higher levels at New Scotland Yard. These meetings had become necessary as a result of the detention of Kelaher by Customs during the Sands enquiry. These meetings would have given the Commissioner an opportunity to criticise Customs for failing to take action against Kelaher and would have offered him the chance to deal with Kelaher.

Our own contacts with Customs were kept to a minimum because of our distrust of them but I later became aware that Kelaher was continually at loggerheads with them as they feared that he was being considered to take up a post as number one to lead operations relating to drug enforcement.

Customs quite rightly would have their nose put out of joint if Kelaher did take up such a position. In view of their investigation into Kelaher, the animosity between them became serious. As to the Home Office, I realised quite early that we had been used by them when they originally asked our team to deal with the so-called celebrities involved in the misuse of drugs. Although we had dealt with a small number of such cases there had never been a big effort to satisfy the Home Office. As a result of information I had received from my contact in the Hong Kong office, I learnt that that department had become aware that our team had decided to scale down our activities against 'possession-only' cases and turn our entire efforts onto drug dealers. This action did not sit well with the Home Office, which did not concern me unduly. Let's be clear about this: to have us arrest John Lennon was their way of keeping us busy. No one wanted us snooping around, and now we knew why. As to the DPP's office, I had little confidence in the decisions that they made when I considered their propensity to make many such decisions on a political basis, as can clearly be seen in the number of long-term cover-ups now coming to light.

The situation in London was malevolent, rotten and inexcusable. I had made the right decision to emigrate and take my family to brighter lands.

Chapter 12
Arrested in Australia

As a result of my decision to resign and move to Perth, we arranged to sell our house and pack our household belongings to be shipped there, which also included our precious dog, a collie named Shep. After a farewell dinner with Nigel, we flew as a family to Singapore, travelling the rest of the way by ship, which took about four days, arriving on the 11th November. It really was quite the adventure. Our departure from the UK had been a heartrending experience as the support given us by our friends both inside and outside of the Force had been overwhelming.

On our arrival in Fremantle harbour aboard the *Eastern Queen*, the ship did not dock but anchored in the middle of the harbour. I was not concerned at that stage but when I saw a tender tie up beside the ship I wondered what was happening. I soon found out when we were approached by two men who identified themselves as CID officers. Life was about to take a very dark and disappointing turn. They had a warrant for my arrest issued by New Scotland Yard. Nothing could have been more of a shock or could have been worse news for me and my family. It begged the question: what on earth?

It was a serious blow to me as all along I did not believe that such action would be taken, not even by Mark in the circumstances surrounding the Salah trial. The two officers involved in my arrest were very worried indeed considering the position of both Shirley and the children, as was I, but they had already arranged accommodation for them, which of course I felt very relieved about. We were taken off the ship and I went to Fremantle Police Station and Shirley and the children went to safe accommodation. They were brilliant officers, which was good because at the time, I was bloody angry. Why bother to let us travel all the way to Australia to arrest us on arrival? Why not just do it back in England? But the reason was immediately clear to me. They wanted it to appear as if I had attempted to do a runner. They wanted me to appear like a Ronnie Biggs.

At the station I had a long discussion with local CID officers and was shown the paperwork submitted by New Scotland Yard for my extradition, including the information submitted to the Guildhall Magistrates Court supporting their case, part of which is shown as follows:

> The evidence against the Salah family consisted to a large extent of evidence of their alleged conversations with police officers, and of observations of their movements sworn to by police officers. It transpired in the course of the trial that there were very many discrepancies between the officers' notebooks and evidence on one hand and their diaries on the other hand. Following the conclusion of the trial an extensive investigation has been undertaken which had revealed that much of the evidence given by the police of observations kept by them was false. Charges 2 to 12 are selected from amongst a larger number of cases where it can be shown that lies were told…

> In addition to those specific offences of perjury in relation to observations, there is a wealth of evidence indicating that there was an agreement amongst all 6 officers to deceive the court about their diary entries. Miss McGibbon appears to have fabricated a notebook for use at the trial, and Victor Kelaher tried to assist his officers when they were caught lying by claiming that he had given instructions to them to falsify their diary entries…

> When interviewed by me, Kelaher constantly made reference to a telephone intercept which was kept on John Salah's calls, saying that it would greatly assist his defence. I have been informed by counsel that a perusal of the tape record leaves no doubt that the Salahs were guilty of the offences with which they were charged. But the allegation by the prosecution is not that the defendants did not carry out the movements that the officers described, but rather that in many instances the officers did not and could not have seen those movements, and probably reconstructed them as a result of their knowledge of the telephone conversations of the defendants.

To put it bluntly – this was all a load of old cobblers, and the Australians were as livid as I was.

'Is this the way Scotland Yard works?' they asked me, horrified at the process.

Mostly, I could not believe that their case was dependent on such a complete lack of understanding of substantive evidence, but it had happened. The claim that there were many discrepancies between our pocket books and diaries was farcical. We had never denied that the entries in our diaries had been fabricated and that our evidence to the court had been given from our pocket book notes. To suggest that observations had not been kept, but had been written up as a result of the conversations, didn't hold water. If that had been the case, should the alleged meetings not have been kept then the person concerned could have proved that they were elsewhere. The fact was that the Salahs never disputed that such meetings had been kept and the evidence proved that they had purchased and altered the trailer as alleged. As to the information that, apart from Charges 2 and 12, there was a larger number of cases where lies were told: this was nonsense, as no evidence had been provided to substantiate such a claim as it did not exist. As to the charge of conspiring to pervert the course of justice and there being a wealth of evidence to indicate that we had agreed to deceive the court about our diary entries: there was no evidence to suggest any such agreement, as we had never denied that our diary entries were false following my seeking authority to take such action. (To add a charge of conspiracy to the substantive charges is a common practice where a case is weak, as conspiracy is easier to prove.)

As a result of a series of discussions with the local CID they expressed their disbelief that New Scotland Yard had acted as they did. I duly appeared at the local magistrates and was remanded to await the arrival of officers from New Scotland Yard. There was no objection to bail being granted, unusual in these cases, and the officer in the case stated that he had in fact found employment for me in the meantime.

Shirley, myself, my daughter Joanne and son Gregg spent a very pleasant Christmas period in Fremantle, due mainly to the efforts of the local CID who arranged a Christmas party and other celebrations for us, for which I was and always will be eternally grateful. Notwithstanding the problems I faced, we, as a family, enjoyed our stay in Perth but it was imperative that Shirley and the children return to the UK because I had decided, against the advice of the local CID, to return voluntarily. They told me not to go back to London, to remain in Australia, and integrate into society, and that nobody would care, but I thought of Nigel, my old pal, and I decided that I must face the allegations laid against us together. We were a team, and we were to face the music together as a team.

In a further effort to convince me to fight the extradition, the locals told me that the magistrate would not agree to confirm the extradition on the evidence submitted by New Scotland Yard, which was considered not satisfactory, and meanwhile they had organised that job for me at the local hospital. I rather stupidly declined their advice, as I later learned that New Scotland Yard's legal department and the DPP's office had met to discuss further moves in seeking my extradition as the warrant granted could not be used outside Great Britain on the two charges; they were discussing whether further action should be taken to bring me back. With the help of my family in the UK, Shirley, Joanne and Gregg returned to England and stayed with my cousin George.

I was now happy that my family were safe among friends; and I later learned that my former colleagues were supporting them financially, led by my first Detective Sergeant John Callen with whom I had worked in Sidcup.

*

On the 31st January 1973 I was told that two officers had arrived from the UK to interview me. Prior to meeting them, I had a discussion with the local CID. I asked them who they were and it was bad news for me and expressive of Robert Mark's hidden hand. When I was told it was Superintendent Faulkner and Detective Sergeant Sullivan my response was, as I recall: 'Well, they've sent Bill and Ben the Flowerpot Men. I would like one of you to be present because Faulkner is a shitbag and he will go to any lengths to justify his promotion.' They laughed but were concerned as well. Faulkner was a uniformed officer who was working for Mark and he was put there to make sure he was going in the direction Mark wanted, which was to put Kelaher in prison, no matter what.

I was seen by Faulkner who said he had a warrant for my arrest. He asked me if I wished to see the documents, which I declined. Faulkner said that I would be taken back to the UK to face the charges.

'I am not guilty of these charges,' I replied. 'I want you to know that I am not saying anything about that or anything else between here and there.'

I was in Faulkner's custody and arrangements were made to travel to Perth airport. When Faulkner made a move to put me in handcuffs the local CID objected: 'You are not putting those on him while you are in Australia, we will take him to the aircraft and you can take over.' They were good men indeed.

I was driven to Perth airport where I was handed over to Faulkner. I said goodbye to the local CID men for whom I still held a high regard. It was good to know that good men still walked, and we all shared a look, which was a strong one. I could see that they knew what was what and that injustice was real and life was quite brutal. The cuffs were on and one of them said the words: 'Good luck Nobby.' I left them and walked away with Faulkner.

The long flight back to the UK was a silent one during which I contemplated my position. Even at that stage I was not unduly concerned about the situation but I was extremely angry that the actions taken by Robert Mark in his determination to finish Kelaher had led to the rest of the team and my family being put in this position. We had worked damned hard to get the results that we did only to be sacrificed to the egotistical desires of one man and we were nothing to him but food for the dogs.

On our arrival back in the UK, I was taken to Snow Hill Police Station in the City of London, formally charged and later released on bail. I wondered then why the matter was being dealt with in the City police area, a question that I still ponder. I can only think that there was a reason to keep it away from the Met, perhaps because there, there was a deep feeling of resentment about the case.

The Salahs were drug dealers and had been found guilty. The evidence for their criminal activities was simply overwhelming but Mark wanted Kelaher and that meant my time in the sunshine was over even before it had begun. I flew to Australia with my family to make a new beginning, and because of him, I had to come back in handcuffs. Because of Kelaher, five of us were about to lose our careers. No more work, no more camaraderie, no more sunshine. There was only prison now on the horizon. But at the time, I was prepared to return and face the music. Was this really all happening? I chose to believe that the truth would set us all free and I knew that Nigel, Nick, Morag and the others would agree. But we would need to get ourselves into good spirits first and that meant a regroup.

Chapter 13
The Trial Part I:
All the World's A Stage

It was an emotional moment when the old Whispering Squad got together again, this time in very different circumstances. I'll let my old friend and colleague Nigel Lilley take up this part of the story:

'We were all in contact with each other at this time and we had to be quite careful because we knew that our phones were being tapped. I phoned Morag and Adam and Nick, and Morag phoned Vic and said, I've got to get hold of Norman. This was about a week or so after Nobby had brought his whole family back. We all got together for the first time in Morag's flat in Richmond Road and said to each other, right, what are we going to do? Our first remand hearing was two weeks away. We basically sat down with the different lawyers present and worked out what we needed to do and how we were going to do it. And the first thing I did, when we all sat down together again for the first time, was to thank Norman for coming back from Australia. He didn't have to come back, he could have stayed out there. Norman told us that the Aussies had said to him that he should stay out there, resist the extradition. But he said there was no way he was going to do that; he didn't even consider it.

'So after that, for the next eighteen months or so, we had fortnightly meetings together to discuss what was happening, how we were reacting to all the different statements being served on us. We were all at different stations by that stage and we had a huge amount of support from other police officers. And we didn't feel downhearted: we all felt that it was a clear, total case of injustice and that we had a complete response to all the allegations. Through Kelaher, we had a number of senior officers coming forward talking about having to make different entries in pocket books for operational reasons, because of the constant suspicions about leaks from inside, so we were comfortable about all that aspect. We all felt positive, even though our lawyer Chris Morris prepared us for the possibility that we might go down, and we were all just getting on with our lives, assuming this would be done and dusted soon.

'But it was a tremendous strain, particularly on our wives and loved ones. Remember, we were on half-wages during all this, so we all had to do outside work just to keep bread on our tables. We were waiting, waiting… you couldn't make any long-term plans, you just had to live from day to day and keep going. We had eighteen long months of that.'

*

After many months of meetings with our legal representatives Kingsley Napley Solicitors, we came to the appointed day to start our trial. My direct contact with Kingsley Napley was Christopher Murray who I had known for many years. This, in my view, was a top-class firm whom I was confident would look after my best interests.

On Friday 17th September 1973 the trial was due to start in Number 1 Court at the Old Bailey, also known as the Central Criminal Court. This was a court in which I had myself appeared on numerous occasions in the past, suffice to say not in the situation I now found myself. I met up with Nigel, Nick, Morag, Adam and Vic Kelaher, all of whom I found to be in good spirits. There were also a large number of our former colleagues who wished us all the very best of luck. Large numbers of the press were present who obviously saw a good story in the making.

Now would be a good time to outline the main actors appearing in this 'show' – one that had been written and choreographed by Robert Mark in cooperation with the DPP's office, the Home Office and Customs and Excise. I had always considered that these courts resembled a stage on which the barristers were the actors who played to an audience, the jury, and the lead was of course the judge. This position was taken by the Right Honourable Mr Justice Melford- Stevenson, before whom I had had the dubious privilege of appearing on two previous occasions. He was a hard man who took a line and kept to it, the ideal person to ensure that this would go the way that he wanted. The truth thus set aside for now. The main supporting actors were the various counsel on view. The prosecution was led by Mr B Leary who had a very strange habit of opening a question with the words, 'How comes it…?' He was assisted by Mr Tudor-Price. The defence were as follows:-

I was represented by Mr Shields QC and Mr Bevan who I had known for many years

Nick was represented by Mr Howard QC and Mr Gardner

Nigel was represented by Mr Parker QC and Mr Boal who I also knew

Adam was represented by Mr Shindler QC and Mr Auds

Morag was represented by Miss Southworth QC and Mr Robinson

Vic Kelaher was represented by Mr Martin QC and Mrs Shaw

As can be seen, these were top class barristers, most of whom sat as judges themselves.

The various charges were put to us and we all pleaded not guilty to a total of twelve counts and it then came to the selection of a jury. There was a list of fifty prospective jurors, all of whom could be objected to by the defence. Our defence counsel thought it advisable to screen the jurors which as we will see – was not a bad idea at all. New Scotland Yard were contacted and asked to carry out Criminal Record Office (CRO) checks on the fifty jurors listed. The response from CRO was that of the total of fifty names submitted, 80 per cent were named in records held at New Scotland Yard! The circus had come to town! As you can imagine, we were completely taken aback by this news. It was not usual practice to carry out these checks but it would have been unfortunate to discover later that a member of the jury had criminal convictions. We were told later that one man in fact had eleven convictions. Like I've always said, it was an orchestrated set-up, amateur hour and it was already pandemonium. We had not even begun!

The farce of jury selection continued, resulting in *five* being excused for family reasons and thirty-three being refused based on our objections. It was eventually agreed that eleven men and one woman would decide our future. The final actors in this saga were:-

Morag accused of one charge of perjury

Nick accused of two charges of perjury

Nigel accused of two charges of perjury

Adam accused of three charges of perjury

And myself accused of three charges of perjury

Together with Vic Kelaher, we were all charged with one charge of conspiracy. Morag – an outstanding investigator who was greatly admired by all – was a privilege to work alongside. The fact was that Morag would have reached the higher levels in the service, and this opportunity was about to be pulled from under her. Nick? He had been promoted to Detective Sergeant, which was affirmation of his ability to make the right decisions in the most difficult situations. He had been our undercover officer and often found himself in dangerous situations, which he dealt with confidently. And Nigel? He was one of a kind, a confident, articulate man with a strong character, which was reflected in his work. His knowledge of the West End was inexhaustible, especially when dealing with the so-called upper crust of society. He was vastly experienced, having dealt with incidents that would have tested the very best of investigators. He was a gentleman and he was my friend. Adam joined our team at a time when we were working around the clock. He rolled up his sleeves, never refusing to work long hours, which hardened him up to deal with what was becoming a dangerous world. Adam belonged to a very upper class family who were exceptionally nice people and whom I had had the pleasure of meeting.

And me? Norman Pilcher? I was my father's son and that felt good to me. Anyway, here we all were. We had lived through some tough and serious work together. Was it always perfect between us all? Of course not. Was the integrity of any of my team ever in question? No. We were a good unit, and we served the public sincerely, with a genuine commitment to bringing drugs off the streets and out of homes and to stop people going in the direction of my friend Tubby Hayes. It was an honour and a privilege to serve but here we stood, beside Vic Kelaher facing charges. He was our Detective Chief Inspector, and was a one-off but too secretive in nature. I guess that was the real sign of his character. Why did you not open up, Vic? Why did you not want to bond? We eventually all found out why, and our shields of denial broken open with a battering ram.

I regarded the team as the best in the service, not one of us ever taking off our full holiday allowance, and working hours that would frighten the life out of most and we showed a loyalty to the Met which was on occasion recognised by senior officers who depended on teams like ours to maintain their own positions and that meant in this instance, sending us to prison.

*

During his opening speech, Mr Leary spoke in a slow and precise manner, not really emphasising salient points. The judge began to ask him to repeat the points and made a great show of writing the points in his notes. This practice was to happen throughout the prosecution case and so I realised at an early stage how I had made quite a serious mistake by not conducting my own defence with the assistance of Chris Murray. Mr Leary made great play of the arrest of Kathleen and Janet in Bulgaria. The fact was that we were disappointed when that happened but no matter how you cut the cake, a large quantity of cannabis had been taken off the streets as a consequence of our work. The team had already gathered overpowering evidence to take action against the Salah family.

The opening speech continued which did nothing in my view to justify the actions taken against our team. Mr Leary suggested that the defence at the Salah trial had got hold of our diaries. I believe that the defence had received information regarding our false entries in those diaries from someone involved in the case. The entries made in our diaries during the Salah investigation were deliberately falsified in order to mislead the mole responsible for leaking our information. The claim by Mr Leary that we had taken this action because of the Salah enquiry was wrong – it had been decided to take such action in 1970 because of leakages to the press. We were frustrated, agitated and already concerned.

On the second day of the trial, the case was moved to Number 8 Court where Mr Leary continued outlining the prosecution case. It was clear that the bulk of his case was related to entries made in the office Day Books and our own entries in our diaries, which did not tie up with our notes in our pocket books. In all but one count of perjury there was direct evidence that we had not been present at the quoted observations. Mr Leary's claim was that we had received the information about the Salah's meetings from the intercept recordings and written up our pocket books without being at the scene. It was patently ridiculous. It would have been possible that such meetings were not kept and the Salah's could have been proved to be elsewhere. In fact the meetings had been kept; this not being disputed. Witnesses for the prosecution were mainly senior police officers who in general outlined police procedures.

Commander Virgo was called and questioned in detail about the procedure for keeping diaries and office Day Books. When he was asked about our being authorised to make false entries in these books, he failed to answer as to whether or not such authority had been given. He only outlined the instructions in general orders relating to the keeping of personal diaries.

When asked whether or not authorisation had been given or if he was aware of the situation, he repeatedly avoided a direct answer, despite him being in full awareness of the actions we were taking. The fact that Virgo was insisting that officers would only enter truthful facts in their diaries was farcical and showed in the eleventh hour his true character through and through. The keeping of diaries has always been a chore and any resemblance to the true movements of officers being recorded was certainly laughable. Virgo had retired from the service at this stage and his appearance gave rise to a comment from Adam – 'He looks like Colonel Blimp'. I must admit that I found it difficult to remember him as the Number One at C1. He was, quite frankly, a disgrace.

After my transfer to New Scotland Yard and C1 Drugs, I was soon aware that there existed an ingrained culture of dark practices It was well known that the Obscene Publications office (the 'Dirty Squad') was a channel through which cash was passed between criminals, who controlled the pornographic trade in London, and certain corrupt police officers. As a result of media investigative work it soon fell upon Robert Mark to deal with the matter. This was an ideal opportunity to enhance his reputation which resulted in a number of very senior officers with the rank of Commander and below being prosecuted for corruption. Following lengthy trials at the Old Bailey, heavy prison terms were passed on those concerned, including Wally Virgo.

Virgo had given evidence for the prosecution in our trial. As the direct result of evidence given by him, which related to the keeping of diaries, he was instrumental in part in our conviction: a senior officer who over many years had been involved in the most serious of corrupt practices. On appeal, Virgo's conviction and sentence were quashed on the technicality of misdirection in the summing up by the trial judge. A number of police witnesses were put forward including Detective Inspector Joe Bolton, a very well-versed officer in relation to drug enquiries. He tried throughout his evidence to distance himself from the Salah enquiry. As the officer running that enquiry, I knew that Bolton had been closely involved in actions taken in the enquiry and as a result of close questioning by the defence counsel, it was clear that Bolton was endeavouring to keep himself out of the frame when it came to those to be prosecuted. The fact was that he was later promoted to Detective Chief Inspector, so make of that what you will.

Another witness called was Detective Chief Superintendent O'Connell – a very highly respected officer who recalled working at C8, the Flying Squad, engaged at racecourses and dealing with gangs of pickpockets. He became convinced that his activities were leaked to these gangs. On one occasion he did enter false information in the duty book as to his movements, which proved successful. It appeared to all of us in the dock that the prosecution were putting forward witnesses who, when put under pressure by defence counsel, did very little to support the prosecution case. Another witness – Detective Sergeant Dudley – had worked on our team for a short period during the Salah enquiries. He admitted that on one occasion he had been engaged on observations at The Meads, Stoke Poges but had shown in the duty book as being in Loughton, Essex. At this stage in the prosecution case, the pendulum had swung in our direction.

As far as Nigel and I were concerned, the case against us rested on an observation that we kept on the 19th January. A Customs officer named Barry Cockerell stated that Nigel had been in his company at the time he said he was on the observation. Nigel had joined up with two Custom officers, Cockerell and Newson, who had intercepted a package containing cannabis. The plan was that a postman would deliver the package to the recipient and they would then enter the address. Nigel, Cockerell and Newson entered the address where they saw a woman, Mrs Oddy, who was questioned by the Customs officer about the cannabis. I could not understand why Nigel had even been told to assist these Customs officers. I had asked him not to hang around with them as I needed him to assist in the observation I had planned for that morning. So it was no surprise to see Nigel join me very quickly at 5 Middle Green Road to see Kathleen Salah arrive at 9.20am, an incident that we both recorded in our pocket books. Both Customs officers gave evidence that Nigel could not have joined me because of the time element. The evidence given by both Customs officers was entirely untrue.

My hope, of course, is that the reader will ask: why would these Customs officers offer false evidence? What possible motive would they have? The answer is mostly clear. There was a serious problem in this case regarding the animosity between Customs and Excise and the Drugs Squad concerning, in particular, Mr Vic Kelaher. This bad feeling came to a head with Kelaher's involvement with the Sands enquiry carried out by Customs. As previously noted, Customs had made serious errors in not dealing with Kelaher when they detained him originally and failed to take the appropriate action. It was clear that serious concerns had been raised, as outlined in Mr Justice Trapnell's closing speech at the Sands trial, which Robert Mark decided to take control of. It became obvious, when considering the evidence given by the two Customs officers, that we were witnessing a new era of cooperation between the two agencies as demanded by the Home Office; this was clear in the determination of Mark and Customs to finish the career of Kelaher by hook or by crook. As regards this particular charge levelled against Nigel and I, it was shown that our pocket book notes were correct whereas the notes in one of the Custom Officer's book showed that the notes had been erased and entries inserted relating to this case.

At this stage in the prosecution case, it appeared probable that their case was falling apart but they soldiered on, calling a witness from the laboratory named Mr Fryd, supposedly a handwriting expert. He appeared to be confused when giving his evidence, implying that I had tried to forge my own signature or that the signatures were intended to be a joke. Melford Stevenson lost patience with this witness and dismissed him and the prosecution case came to a rather dreary close. Mr Leary had not been a particularly robust prosecutor; he was in fact the fourth choice to lead this case after Mr John Matthew, Mr John Buzzard and Mr Corkery who had prosecuted in the Salah trial. All throughout the prosecution case, Melford-Stevenson made numerous remarks to emphasise points which Mr Leary had failed to push home, whilst making great play of writing notes and looking at the jury. In fact Adam pointed out that his father, who was an experienced magistrate, was extremely angry with Melford Stevenson's attitude, which he said was discourteous. In my opinion the case to that stage had been a farce in the true theatrical sense. Melford Stevenson was gently and constantly guiding and escorting the prosecution through their work. The moment the prosecution seemed to lack in their own certainty or sureness, Melford Stevenson was there to lay a helping hand, as if the prosecution were in acting school, and he, the acting coach, was providing them with the support they needed to get through their performance. Shakespeare was right it seems, that the all the world is a stage. And all the men and women merely players...

If the world is a theatre stage, the courtroom on that particular day was a pretty bad show. Nobody could believe what they were seeing. You couldn't write a comedy script like it. Our human nature was on full display for myself and my team. Not only were some people able to cheat, thieve and fiddle to make money and broker deals, they were able to do it to break lives, shatter homes and engineer social status. It wasn't thieves and pickpockets and dealers on the streets, it was judges, officials and lawyers in the courts all working for the ambitious and progressive Robert Mark.

'Would you like to join the Lodge?' they once asked me.

'No,' I told them. 'I don't like secret societies.'

Perhaps if I had said yes, started scratching backs years before and allowed myself to become unprincipled, promoted up the ranks through unjust means and the secret handshake, I would not have found myself on the receiving end of such hypocrisy. Maybe I would have been able to 'buy' my way out but I would always recall what my father told me: *Show 'em what you're made of*. So if they were going to take me down, I would keep my dignity and not budge an inch from the one thing I came to trust and know as my secret and only real refuge: the truth.

Chapter 14
The Trial Part II:
The Circus Came to Town

Into the third week and the jury were sent home whilst the defence submitted that there was no case to answer as no physical evidence had been forthcoming in order to prove 'perjury'. It was a trial within a trial but at the end of the day, Melford-Stevenson rejected all the submissions. If he had allowed any of the counts to be set aside, the whole case would have collapsed and he had no intention of letting that happen. No doubt Robert Mark would have been pleased at his nightly meeting.

Nick was the first to enter the witness box on the 3rd October. He gave his evidence in reply to questions from his counsel Mr Howard QC after which Mr Leary had his chance to take stage front. He didn't get much joy and Nick finished his evidence after two and a half days.

On the 12th October it was my turn to state exactly how the Salah case was handled. I made it clear that the case had progressed in the same way as all other cases of this nature. I had always enjoyed my sessions in the witness box and this I felt was an occasion where I was expecting Mr Leary to do his best to basically wind me up. After my counsel, Mr Shields QC, had put my defence forward in detail – outlining the manner in which the team had carried out their enquiries, which resulted in the arrests and subsequent convictions of the Salah family – I had to face an intense grilling by Mr Leary, which I found to be lacking in the push and thrust which I had expected. Throughout he was being assisted by Melford-Stevenson who was intent on highlighting salient points to the jury. I remained in the box for three days and was satisfied that the prosecution were finding themselves having serious problems. Nigel followed me into the witness box and I knew that he would acquit himself well and I was not disappointed by his performance. He was confident and polite, keeping control of his temper, something that Mr Leary failed to do on several occasions.

On the seventeenth day of the trial, the 16th October, at the conclusion of the day's business, the jury had left for the day when Mr Leary stated that he had a new statement which he wished the judge to see. Mr Leary was asking that this statement, made by a Mrs Oddy, be allowed in the prosecution case which had been closed several days earlier. Melford-Stevenson had a problem in that he was clearly assisting Mr Leary with his case. The court procedures clearly direct that such evidence must not be allowed unless it is rebuttal evidence which is allowed to refute defence evidence. The problem for Melford-Stevenson was that if he allowed the statement to be entered it would be grounds for an appeal and he would be criticised by the Appeal Court. I later learned that the prosecution had been fully aware that Mrs Oddy had made a statement regarding the visit to her house at Tolworth Rise, Surbiton, by the Customs officers who were following the delivery of the parcel of cannabis. As a result of the differences between the Customs Officer and Nigel regarding the timing of events on that day, it was imperative that Mrs Oddy gave evidence.

Nigel had given evidence that they had arrived at Tolworth Rise at 8.09am but the Customs officers had stated that it was 9.08am. Mrs Oddy was alleged to have returned after taking her child to school at 9.30am but Nigel was in fact with myself in Mapledene Road.

After much debate between the judge, Mr Leary and the defence counsel, it appeared that Melford-Stevenson was doubtful as to its propriety as the prosecution case had been closed. Notwithstanding these doubts, he decided to allow Mrs Oddy to give evidence. The court adjourned for the day with the defence arguing with Mr Leary and the matter ended with much confusion. We all discussed matters regarding the prosecution case and agreed that the probability was that Mr Leary had realised that even with the assistance that he was getting from Melford-Stevenson, the evidence given by the Customs officers was a question of their word against Nigel and myself and so must have raised doubts in the minds of the jury. I later learned that Mrs Oddy had not been called during the prosecution case as it was felt that she did not have a clear recollection of the events of that day or the times involved. I also learned that before Mrs Oddy's appearance in court she had been coached through her evidence. I found Mrs Oddy to be a very pleasant lady who, when in the witness box, appeared quite uncomfortable indeed. Her original statement had been written for her and the times mentioned had been suggested to her by the officers carrying out the interview. It was as clear as a pikestaff that had Mrs Oddy's evidence not been allowed, then the findings in this matter would have been very different. I still do not understand why, if the prosecution really needed confirmation of the disputed times in this matter, they did not question the postman: surely it would have been more reliable to have quizzed he who delivered the parcel? But he was not called and so the question then had to be asked: was he was not called *because* of the fact that he would (very likely) not budge on the timings (which were different to those put forward by the Customs officers)?

The defence continued to put our evidence to the jury, calling us one by one and we were closely questioned by the prosecution in the form of Mr Leary, who, to put it mildly, made a pig's ear of the matter. The prosecution need not have worried as the judge consistently stepped in to help Mr Leary out. A number of witnesses were called on our behalf, many of whom confirmed and verified our evidence relating to the casual manner in which diaries were compiled. The defence evidence in my case lasted over one and a half days during which time it was clearly stated that our team had an exemplary record.

At the conclusion of this evidence, once again, Melford-Stevenson stepped in with a significant comment aimed at the jury: 'There is a well-known saying within these courts that every criminal has to start somewhere.' Did he actually just say that? In a sudden moment, the court was totally silent and the defence barristers were looking at one another in disbelief. Melford Stevenson then quickly adjourned the court for the day. The fact that he had made that remark was simply shocking, and to us, it was a demonstration of how he was running the case.

During the course of Kelaher's defence, mention of his involvement in the Sands case was raised and it was apparent that allegations had been made against him by Customs officers. Further evidence was forthcoming regarding the making of false entries in CID diaries which was supported by senior officers.

The production of all the relevant evidence came to a close after thirty days, leading to the closing speeches of counsel and the summing up by the judge. On the 9th November we sat in the dock with one thought on our minds – that Melford- Stevenson would try to lead the jury by the nose into returning guilty verdicts. We were proved to be right as the judge made every effort to make the prosecution case regarding the count of conspiracy stick. The fact was that there was no substantive evidence that we had put our heads together in a criminal effort to prove our case. As I have noted before, this charge is always put forward when the remaining case is weak. It was purely an effort to involve Kelaher on the instructions of Mark who was addicted to the idea that he had to put Kelaher away. As I learnt, addiction in all its forms is negative and will never produce good results; the desire by Mark would come unstuck.

Melford-Stevenson devoted the latter part of his summing-up to the evidence concerning Kelaher. He only mentioned the case presented by the prosecution and it was very clear that Melford -Stevenson was directing the jury to a guilty finding in the conspiracy count. This was confirmation as far as I was concerned that this whole charade was set in motion to ensure that Kelaher was dealt with. It became necessary for two junior counsels to remind the judge and the court that certain points which favoured the defence had not been mentioned.

The court was adjourned until 10.30am on Tuesday 13th November. Before the judge addressed the jury, Nigel's junior counsel, Mr Graham Boal, made some points to the jury about what two witnesses had said in Nigel's favour which the judge had ignored in his summing up. This intervention was not dealt with by the judge who then invited the jury to retire to consider their verdicts. At this stage it was indeed an interval in the theatre.

The six of us were taken below, Morag to the female section and the rest of us to the male detention room. We were obviously concerned considering the outcome of our situation. Casual conversation was limited but I was very worried about Morag who I felt had been put through enough distress by having to spend a night in Holloway, none of which she deserved.

And then I had a conversation with Vic Kelaher who said what were to be his final words to me, 'Don't worry, there will be no unanimous verdicts.'

I did not know what he meant. I asked him why and he told me:

'Because I have got two in the jury.'

As if life could not have gotten any worse, I suddenly felt sick, and in that moment I realised just what sort of a man Kelaher was once and for all. All my suspicions, confirmed in a heartbeat. Him stating that 'I have got two in the jury' meant that he had personally paid off two people to side with us. I took him to one side as I did not want the others to hear my own final words.

'What the fucking hell have you done now?' I had the man's attention, finally. 'If this comes on top you have put me in it too. There is Morag locked away on her own and us sitting here not knowing what the fuck is going to happen.'

He tried to interrupt me but I talked over him:

'You are the reason we are here, because of Mark's determination to put you away. You should have been in the dock beside Sands and company but because of the incompetence of the Customs you escaped.'

I walked away from Kelaher joining the others who knew that something was very wrong. I realised that the probability was that he had been involved in the Sands case, the result of which had led to our team's present situation. But for the corrupt practices involving Kelaher, the evidence put forward by the prosecution relating to our diaries would at most have to be dealt with as an internal disciplinary matter. I have never spoken to or been in contact with Vic Kelaher again since he made that admission.

Throughout this whole period, I still considered that it was my responsibility to keep the whole show on the road. I had led the Drugs Squad, and in my mind, I still did. While putting this final report together, I asked Nigel Lilley how it had seemed to him, and again, I'll let him do the talking:

'What we were doing in the Drugs Squad wasn't what I would call cops and robbers stuff – you know who the bad guy is, there he is, go and arrest him. We were working at a time, in the 1960s, when the whole world was changing, society was changing and everything was completely different. And the reason for that was music, the arts, films; the Playboy Club had opened, there were all sorts of things happening in society. And the Home Office was charged with doing something, so they said, let's arrest all these pop stars and once they're arrested, then the teenagers won't follow them. But we said amongst ourselves, we don't think it's going to work that way. The badge of honour for kids is going to be getting nicked for drugs. Anyway, very early on, we went out as instructed and did some raids. We all managed to produce some good information and we also seemed to gel as a team, mainly because Norman did what a leader should do, which was, the buck stops here. So if something happens to one of you, or one of you makes a mistake, then it's actually my responsibility and I'll deal with it. That's actually the first rule of leadership. And as a result, there was almost a kind of competition with the other squads: no matter how hard they tried, they never achieved the standards we had. We had really good standards. We had good information, we had a good process, we worked really well as a team, we liked each other, we got on well together, we'd all go out together every so often to the dogs with our wives. More important than any of that though, was that we trusted each other in situations which were generally pretty bloody dangerous, because we were unarmed and usually had absolutely no means of communication with the outside world. We played a very important part, not just within London but also within the Met's dealings with other police forces, the FBI, the CIA and so on. We were relied upon, we played our part, and it was all because Nobby protected us. Because we knew the buck stopped with him, we didn't want to screw up and let him down. It was as simple as that.'

*

After thirty-eight days of the trial, a decision had been made by the jury. It was Wednesday, 14th November 1973, the day that Princess Anne married Captain Mark Phillips. The jury had returned to court and when asked by the clerk of the court whether they had reached a verdict on any count the foreman replied:

'We have.'

The clerk asked: 'Are you agreed?' and the foreman replied, 'We are.'

The clerk then asked:

'Do you find Adam Buzzard Acworth guilty or not guilty on Count 9 of perjury?'

The reply was, 'Not guilty.'

There was a sigh of relief from us and Melford-Stevenson told the jury that he would accept majority decisions on the remaining counts and the jury retired again to consider the other counts on the indictment.

At 2.15pm the court had reassembled when we saw the judge looking at a piece of paper. He gave a long sniff and looked around the court, which was packed to bursting point. Crikey, it was a shock and all the officers were about to feel a real whack as the judge said the words, 'I have received a note which says that the jury have arrived at a further three unanimous verdicts and seven majority verdicts but they are apparently having some difficulty over Count 12, the conspiracy charge. There is some trouble about the interpretation of the last two lines of the indictment as written. That's right isn't it?'

The foreman of the jury nodded and Melford-Stevenson went on to explain the prosecution's case that the alleged instructions by Kelaher and myself regarding the security situation were not in fact given. The jury had to decide whether or not there was a conspiracy and the jury retired again.

The jury returned having made their decisions. The clerk then asked the foreman of the jury, a man named Cyril Barnes, if they had reached verdicts on the remaining counts.

'We have,' replied Mr Barnes.

The jury had been out for a total of eleven hours and fifty-five minutes. The clerk said to Mr Barnes:

'Will you answer as I put the charges to you?'

Clerk:	'Do you find Adam Buzzard Acworth guilty or not guilty on Count 1?'
Foreman:	'Not guilty.'
Clerk:	'Do you find Morag McGibbon guilty or not guilty on Count 2?'
Foreman:	'Not guilty.'
Clerk:	'Do you find George Nicholas Prichard guilty or not guilty on Count 3?'
Foreman:	'Guilty by a majority of ten to two.'
Clerk:	'Do you find Norman Clemence Pilcher guilty or not guilty on Count 4?
Foreman:	'Guilty by a majority of ten to two.'
Clerk:	'Do you find George Nicholas Prichard guilty or not guilty on Count 5?'
Foreman:	'Not guilty.'
Clerk:	'Do you find Adam Buzzard Acworth guilty or not guilty on Count 6?'
Foreman:	'Not guilty.'
Clerk:	'Do you find Norman Clemence Pilcher guilty or not guilty on Count 7?'
Foreman:	'Guilty by a majority of eleven to one.'
Clerk:	'Do you find Nigel Patrick Lilley guilty or not guilty on Count 8?'
Foreman:	'Guilty by a majority of eleven to one.'

On Count 12, which referred to all of us, conspiracy to pervert the course of justice, the jury returned a verdict of not guilty unanimously. The court was suddenly deafening with one woman openly crying and clearly saying the words, 'It's so unfair'. The foreman asked the judge if the jury could add a rider to their verdicts and said that as far as the three who had been guilty were concerned, the jury took the view that the offences were of a minor nature and not undertaken in any spirit of malice.

'In view of the past records of the accused we ask you to deal with them with the utmost leniency.'

The defence asked that Adam, Morag and Kelaher be discharged, which they were.

Melford-Stevenson now had the task of pronouncing sentence on Nigel, Nick and myself bearing in mind the remarks made by the jury. He sentenced Nigel and Nick to eighteen months imprisonment each and turned to me. I knew that he was distraught that for all his efforts he had failed in his quest to get Kelaher convicted. I knew that he would disregard the jury's views and that I would be in for a tough time. Sure enough, he made the usual speech about the evil actions involved in the case. The end result was that he sentenced me to four years on each count meaning that I would serve four years. This meant that the record could not be regarded as a 'spent' record, it would remain with me for life – a nasty little dig at me by Melford-Stevenson who was personally resentful at the acquittal of Kelaher. Although I was very depressed at the result for Nigel, Nick and myself, I felt that a huge load had been lifted from my shoulders with the acquittals of Morag and Adam.

*

The conspiracy charge that was brought against me and my team was a joke, so Mark's mission to take us out to get to Kelaher was never going to work. And it didn't work. We were on our way to prison, and Kelaher was going free. Mark just couldn't let it go. Most won't know it but if you're doing a big enquiry, you always stick on a conspiracy charge because that's the easy one in the world to prove, so that's always the sign that the whole thing is clutching at straws.

Do you know what the biggest irony of all was? Even right at the end, Kelaher was getting inside information. He told me at the trial, right at the time when he blurted out to me about his alleged jury nobbling, that a contact of his had been told that Melford-Stevenson had been bragging about the upcoming trial at, of all places, a health farm. According to Kelaher, the judge had told two women who were also at the health farm: 'Don't worry, I'm going to get Kelaher.' Well, he failed in that, didn't he?

Mark was asked about the enquiry at the time and if he felt it fair that he was involving my team in his investigation. His response was as noted and one I will never forget and one worth repeating, for my own process and for the record:

'I want Kelaher in prison. They're just collateral damage.'

They were his words. Solid words that underlined his unshakeable commitment to his mission. He really did hold the obsession of a maniac.

They were going to discipline Kelaher on a list a mile long but like a coward, he ducked out on ill health. In one way, Mark had achieved something, in that he got him out of the job, but he didn't achieve what he wanted in putting him behind bars. The trial was based on the use of our diaries and the sore point was that I and my team asked for permission to put false entries in, of which we were granted authorisation. And that's what they came after us for. Normally people don't ask permission to put false entries in, they just do it. We asked, and were given permission, and they took us down for it. As I have explained: the end justifies the means. We were given permission to use false entries by Kelaher, and then by Virgo, who told us to 'Do what ya gotta do.' I was quite relaxed throughout our trial because I had nothing to be concerned about; but I was naïve about the level of false virtue endemic in the Met.

We were going away and Kelaher was laughing. Did Mark get his comeuppance? I don't know but I'd like to think that somehow these sorts of things balance out, like the angels balance things out for us somehow, in a faraway place.

In hindsight, I'm glad I spoke my truth and did the years in prison so I can sit here today and look back on it all knowing what I know, that my team were straight and that those who put us away only highlighted the fact that we were. Perhaps at the time I should have defended myself but hindsight, as they say, is a wonderful thing.

I was about to reflect on it all, get my mind straight on matters and understand more deeply the nature of how things were playing out... behind bars.

Chapter 15
Prison!

As a result of the circus act witnessed at the Old Bailey, Nigel, Nick and I were in the uncomfortable position of finding ourselves in prison.

We had been moved to Ford Open Prison in Sussex and this was to be our home for some time; but I believe that we had the right attitude, which was to take every day as it came. It began for us in a rather entertaining way.

'K Hut,' a voice called out, 'stand up and listen.' The voice was commanding, so we all did stand. In fact, the voice could not have been more deafening and booming, with the power of a male soprano he immediately held the attention of the room.

'I know these gentlemen,' and he was pointing at Nigel, myself and Nick, and with a terrific presence that had a definite authority,

'And I know *that* gentleman Mr *Lilley* very, *very* well. And I call him Mr. Lilley because I have total respect for him.' All were silent as he spoke. 'He arrested me and treated me with respect and I hope that nobody here will treat him with disrespect,' he nodded and marched out of the room.

We had no intention of moping about complaining. We all wanted to do things and contribute. I soon realised that Ford was more like a holiday camp than a place of confinement. On the contrary, anyone could pretty much walk out at any time. You wouldn't need to tunnel under! We soon settled in, having no problems from the other residents and we were all given what we thought were good positions.

I was responsible for looking after the needs of the Welfare Officers, which enabled me to move around the estate as I liked. This setup eased my depression at having been put there which was denying me the right to be with Shirley, Joanne and Gregg and not being able to provide for them. I did know that they were looked after by former colleagues, a fact that I was to become eternally grateful for. The fact was that we were being punished in not being with our families but this was eased slightly because of the conditions at Ford. To be quite honest, it was like a script from *Porridge* most days! There were even occasions when men who were being released would punch out the officers to try and stay a while longer! All round, the prison staff were friendly and not too interested in enforcing the rules. It would have been easy to simply walk out of prison at any time but such an action would have meant being returned to a closed prison on re-arrest, so it was an incentive to stay and see the term out. Whilst incarcerated at Ford I played football in the local league and studied to become a qualified referee together with playing cricket, again in the local league. All in all life was not too bad; after all, who can boast of having played cricket at Arundel Castle?

It was not long before I had a visit from Detective Chief Superintendent Mees who was looking at other cases that we had dealt with. I obviously insisted that Prison Officers were present in these meetings, which centred on anything I knew about Kelaher's activities. Because of Kelaher's habit of keeping things to himself, I couldn't offer any assistance to Mees, not that I would have done so had I been able to. In fairness to Mees he did say that he was very sorry to see us in our situation but that he had been 'between a rock and a hard place' while engaged on the enquiry. I remember very clearly that he put his hand on my shoulder and said the words directly,

'I'm sorry Nobby but you know very well that Kelaher was who Mark wanted.'

It seemed that Mark was still after him, as if there was a greater reason for his private vendetta.

*

As a result of the conduct of Melford-Stevenson during the trial, an appeal was lodged on behalf of Nigel, Nick and myself. This appeal was primarily due to the decision of Melford-Stevenson to allow the evidence of Mrs Oddy to be put forward after the closing of the prosecution case. Such action went against the rules of evidence. The Appeal Court judges decided that Melford-Stevenson had been wrong to allow the evidence to be put forward and at that stage our appeal would normally have been allowed but as usual the establishment had a 'get out of trouble card' up their sleeves. It was apparently, a 'proviso' which allowed the Appeal Court to override the deliberate wrong decision made by Melford-Stevenson and reject the appeal. Apparently, they decided that the jury would have reached the same verdicts without Mrs

Oddy's evidence. I have never understood how three High Court judges can read the minds of jurors. Anyway the die was cast and we would have to see out our time. Some inmates were in fact happy to serve their time and on many occasions we saw men being carried out of there. They were in fact so comfortable that they would choose to be there than face the real world!

Time passed quickly during which we had some hilarious episodes, like when we were due to play cricket in Arundel. Our transport in the form of a minibus was packed with our cricket gear and off we went. We hadn't travelled far when the bus left the road with the front wheel stuck in a ditch. The officer driving was slumped over the wheel, obviously the worse for drink. We discussed what to do and decided to walk to Arundel to play our match. The driver was alright and would soon wake up. There was the sight of a dozen men clad in white walking into Arundel to play cricket. During the course of the match our driver arrived to find his flock all present and correct. As with all prisons, the inmates will always find ways to outfox the staff. The residents of Ford were no exception as the staff just wanted a quiet life –their conditions of employment were excellent when compared to those in closed institutions. It was common practice for us to pop out in the evening to a local pub for a drink and the staff were very helpful when visits were made, usually once a month. Shirley and the children were always catered for during their visits.

After about nine months both Nigel and Nick were released to rebuild their lives, which they did in outstanding style. The day Nigel left his girlfriend picked him up in a convertible Rolls Royce! The time had flown by but I was forced to remain in the camp after Nigel and Nick had left and the extra time soon began to drag; but soon enough, I was allowed to re-join Shirley, Joanne and Gregg. Nigel picked me up that day and brought me home, because he had been paying me visits. It was lovely to be back with them all. It was like coming out of the army, only a hundred times better because the punishment in going to prison for me was that I lost my right to provide for my family. I had missed them dearly, but now I was back.

I immediately went into full time employment whilst I sorted out where our futures lay. The probation service sorted out a job and I began working with the London Electricity Board, checking customers' accounts. I was bored to tears but they were very good. We moved into a new house where life settled down into a routine but I missed the hustle and bustle of my previous existence. I started a driving school to put me in contact with the public again but nothing was ever the same as working in the Force.

There was an event which happened a few weeks after my release. We were at home in the evening when there was a knock at the door. I answered and was surprised to find one of my former colleagues on the doorstep who enquired into how we were. He asked me if I could look after a package which contained paperwork relating to an enquiry that he had recently been involved with. He said that he was expecting to be 'turned over' and his house searched and he didn't want the papers to be found. Like an old fool, I agreed to look after the parcel and he left. I was then faced by Shirley who was very angry indeed.

'What have you done, you silly man?'

I realised that I had been caught off-guard and could indeed find myself in a very difficult situation. I had done something quite stupid, Shirley was right, for it could have been a stitch-up. I didn't know what was in the parcel so I decided to return the package but to put my own mind at rest I decided to see what the package contained. A quick examination revealed a large amount of bank notes. 'Sugar, if there are people outside filming I'm done for,' I said to my wife who was stood with arms crossed. 'They might come knocking in a minute!' I went straight to my former colleague's address in Sidcup where the door was answered by his wife who I knew. I handed her the package requesting that she tell her husband to stay away from me and not to contact me again, ever. I returned home to a very frosty welcome from my wife.

'Daft old bugger,' she said to me.

I realised the position I had put myself in and contacted Chris Murray who had been looking after my affairs. After I had outlined the event to him, he suggested that he contact senior counsel for advice. Chris later contacted me to pass on the advice put forward by a leading Treasury Counsel, which was to contact the enquiry team at New Scotland Yard. I decided not to deal with it in that way but visited Chris Murray's office with Shirley the following day to submit statements regarding the matter. As to the colleague who had put me in that position: it was clear that he had been involved in corrupt practices and had been ready to involve me. I later learned that he eventually retired as a detective superintendent. His attempt to frame me was truly wicked.

I have spent the last forty years in various businesses, which have been interesting without being stressful. I still read with interest the volumes of what can only be called 'literary garbage' relating to our work on the Drugs Squad. I read an article posted on a well-known informative website that I had passed away in 2011 in Eastbourne Hospital which I found to be quite hilarious of course.

During the late eighties I was in a business involved in catering. It was whilst I was attending a function in London and enjoying the usual canapes and white wine when I was approached by a man, who I did not know. He introduced himself, asking if I was Nobby Pilcher. I quite naturally was always very wary of strangers, but reluctantly admitted that I was the one and same person. The man went on to say that he was pleased to see me after so many years as he had been a member of the jury involved in my trial. I remember a warning bell sounding in my head and feeling that I would rather have been *anywhere* but in this very spot. I tried to move on but the man was intent on talking to me. I realised that there was no escape so we sat down for a drink. He told me that he had regretted for many years having been part responsible for the outcome of the trial. He said that at one point in the case, after the prosecution had finished, the jury had a discussion as to whether they should request that the trial be *stopped* as they were not satisfied with the prosecution case which relied on the evidence of the Customs officers – it amounted to their word against that of the police. He explained that they decided to let the case continue, but that had they realised that the defence counsel had also made an application along the same lines, they would have requested that the case be stopped.

At this stage in the conversation I was beginning to get quite angry – I really didn't want to hear these facts after what we had been put through. He went on to say that the evidence given by Mrs Oddy had swung the case against us. I told him that the court of appeal had decided that her evidence should not have been allowed as part of the prosecution case. The judge was criticised by the appeal court but they decided to reject the appeals, obviously saying that the jury would have reached the same guilty verdicts. When I told him *that* he became very upset and wanted to know how judges sitting in the appeal court could decide how the minds of a jury worked. I did not want to continue this conversation so I remember saying to him that had the jury bothered to read between the lines in the case maybe they would have reached a *just* conclusion. I left the man to his own thoughts, hoping that I had not salved his conscience.

Chapter 16
Was I The Walrus?

I have to assess just how much I learned during the seventeen years of service in the Metropolitan Police. I most certainly realised very quickly that the men and women who staffed the service were, in the main, good honest people who found great satisfaction in dealing with the public. Unfortunately there is a very small percentage of officers who find that their positions offer them the opportunity to act in a corrupt manner. They allow themselves to be corrupted. There is a well-quoted saying that 'Every society gets the police it deserves.' I would agree with this in that, over the past decades, policing has changed because criminal behaviour has become increasingly violent. In order to deal with the current situation it has meant that whereas the officer on the beat in the 1960s would carry out his everyday duties equipped with a whistle and truncheon, the officer today walks the streets in a high visibility jacket, a stab vest, truncheon, handcuffs, radio, on-person camera and probably more. During my service in uniform I never had occasion to draw my truncheon. Whilst in the CID I never carried a truncheon or was equipped with handcuffs.

Taking this matter further, officers are seen on the streets looking as if they are expecting a firefight to erupt. These changes in our police service are necessary in view of the upsurge in violence on our streets. There are significant changes in the way that criminal offences are investigated, certainly since the early 1970s. Prior to that, the investigator had the assistance of fingerprint and blood analysis plus the evidence of verbal reports submitted by the investigators. They now have DNA, digital, photographic and scientific evidence to prove their case, which has meant a high rate of convictions, especially historic cases which have lain dormant for years.

I have over the past four decades taken a keen interest in the level of alleged corruption within the Met. During the reign of Robert Mark as Commissioner, great play was made by the media of his 'success' in eradicating alleged corruption in the Force. The figures of over 300 detectives leaving gave the impression this was due to Mark's crackdown. Nothing could be further from the truth. The fact was that many of those mentioned took early retirement because they could not continue serving under Mark. A large number of valued, experienced detectives were lost to public companies including the finest senior officer I had the pleasure of knowing, Iain Forbes, an officer with an unrivalled record. Robert Mark could claim that he had changed the police during his period in office but this would be only his ego. The records show that Mark had, during his early years, an excellent record as an active police officer rising to the rank of Chief Constable but everything appeared to have changed after his period as 'bag man' to Lord Mountbatten. It would seem that Mark had become aware that his own ambitions would be best served if he became politically oriented, as the politicians were gradually taking control over the police service nationally. Mark certainly chose the right route to take as he soon became the so-called 'Top Cop' in the UK. On his eventual retirement, Mark was heaped with praise by the media over his apparent cleansing of the Met but the post-Mark period shows clearly that corruption was even deeper ingrained within the specialist departments. The evidence to support this claim has been well documented in a number of publications, one of which is *Untouchables,* written by Michael Gillard and Laurie Flynn who have written in great detail about the extensive corruption in various specialist squads.

I do not dispute the fact that numerous Chief Officers of Police have endeavoured to eradicate the source of corruption over the decades but without any notable success. History shows that since the raising of a regulated police service in 1829 and the creation of a Detective Department in 1842, corruption has been present together with the toxic influence of Freemasonry. Many worthy officers have endeavoured to uncover the true level of wrongdoing in the service and one such officer was Reginald Morrish who served from 1911 until 1937 in various ranks, retiring as a Chief Inspector. Morrish disregarded the opposition to his work by fellow officers and never gave way to threats that he was subjected to. His activities came to the notice of Lord Trenchard who fully supported his work. Morrish came to the firm conclusion that the corruption was closely connected to the membership of both officers and criminals to the Freemasons.

The area of public service lends itself to corrupt practices and once again the toxic influence of the Freemasons comes into play. Throughout all areas of public service – civil service, legal profession, armed services and the law enforcement agencies – membership of the Society of Freemasonry is deemed to be an asset to seeking advancement. This especially applies to the police service in which membership of a secret society should be known, if not banned entirely; but surely it should be required that such membership should be registered with the employer? Research into many serious cases of alleged corruption over the past 150 years has shown that the influence of the Freemasons was present in such cases. An example of this is that in one particular crime squad in South London, which was the subject of serious allegations of corrupt practices, virtually all the staff were members of one Lodge. One Detective Constable held the position of Master of the Lodge. He subsequently committed suicide whilst under investigation. It was a great help to any officer seeking to climb through the ranks to be able to offer the magic handshake when appearing before a selection board. I can say that during my period of service I saw many individuals move up through the ranks, on the work of others, having no real experience of real policing or common sense and becoming administrators concerned only with their own self-advancement. It's a bad system based not on real knowledge and understanding, and one driven by ambition, greed, fear and self-protection.

As I have noted before, the police service has changed since the '70s. The illusion that the service is independent of political influence is of course now dead and buried. Therefore in order to re-establish the public's confidence in their police service, politicians must take the bull by the horns in order to offer a service that is fit for purpose in the twenty-first century. A step in the right direction must be to follow Scotland and to install a police service for England and Wales. The county force system is no longer fit for purpose. It is no longer acceptable that different areas work to different working practices, separate systems of purchasing equipment, all of which would be better controlled centrally.

*

I round off my remarks over the previous pages by stating with all of my strength that the Metropolitan Police is without doubt comprised of fine men and women who devote their lives to public service. They have been let down by poor leadership which allows corrupt practices to fester. In the many incidents involving serious allegations it is very rare to see the internal enquiries resulting in prosecutions. This is due in the main to the determination of senior officers to cover up malpractice in order to maintain their own positions. This is not a problem applying only to the Met, it is endemic in law enforcement agencies.

Surely it is not beyond the capabilities of those in power to devise systems that will act as checks on the actions of all in public service? A strict system would not cause problems with the vast majority who work within the rules. I can say from my own experience that had I been able to avail myself of a check under a polygraph examination, none of our team would have suffered as we did.

In closing this narrative I wish to pay tribute to all of the officers, both uniform and CID, with whom I worked and became life-long friends. Back then, working as an investigator was hard work. Nowadays with all the technology, it's a bit easier and they don't have to rely too much on how they deal with an offender. Now it's all about DNA, photographs and tapes. We didn't have any of these things in our day but good luck to them if they can get good honest results. It really has changed completely.

Due to the writings of people like Simon Wells, I became a folklore bogeyman to a collective youth who needed and desired an enemy of the times. As the years swung by, I observed this happen naturally as if from the shadows of an ignorant but enthusiastic public. Unbeknownst to them, they read cheap media based on rumour and hearsay and such Chinese whispers create phony and fake stories. Unfortunately for some, this straight and narrow memoir will likely disappoint. The enemy thus created from a rebellious culture was in fact a normal man, working an honest day; a policeman who, funnily enough, didn't like to drink too much. This may all come as a disappointment but I was not bent, I was not corrupt and I was not responsible for many of the arrests claimed. Was I deserving of this reputation? Probably not. Was I the Walrus? Actually... I don't know! You decide. I suppose it is entirely possible.

Regarding Kelaher? And what happened to me? Going to prison? As I reflect back on it now, with that bit of hindsight, I think to myself: that was my career that was ruined. I'd have kept developing and providing good work through the force if I was allowed to. I used to wake up in the morning and I couldn't *wait* to get to work. I used to think to myself, not two minutes ago I was stood there on the steps outside Peel House. I loved it all deeply and truly. It was one of those sorts of jobs and to me, that's how it *was* but that was taken away from me. Looking back, knowing what I do, I feel absolutely furious that that was taken from me and I see it happen to so many people who have been in the same position – really hard grafters who have worked who suddenly find that they get to a level where the people at the top feel that these hard grafters are dangerous and threatening to the status quo, and they like to make things difficult for these gems. Sadly they eventually resign because they're sick of it and this is what happens.

Unfortunately, it is the way the culture is, and I want to see it broken by exposing the Masons. I want to see the influence of them disappear. If you are in public service and you join Freemasonry, you should declare it but they don't. It's a secret society and I'm sure they're not all bad. I am sure there are some good blokes in it too, but that is beside the point, entirely. There are certain groups who wheel and deal to their own advantage and I dread to think what goes on behind these closed doors. What are they keeping secret? And if it's not a big deal, why all the secrecy? The MPs who make the rules are all Freemasons and they're not going to do anything because they are comfortable existing how they do – which is outside of the law, in the same way the mafia work. In the legal profession, especially, they wheel and deal together. It's frightening and creepy beyond words. The worse thing of all? That good men and women suffer as a result of their schemes and plans.

*

When we turned that corner and finally brought the Home Office into our way of thinking, that we should be going after the traffickers, we gained a lot of respect, having seized a large amount of drugs. The Bureau for Narcotics and Dangerous Drugs in the States wanted to work with us; the FBI, the CIA, they all used to come over and work with us; the Canadians – the Royal Canadian Mounted Police (RCMP) – they all used to come and see us. We did a lot of observation of suspects for them all around the world, from South America across to Turkey through the European centres. There was an amazing gathering of trafficking routes found by my team, some fantastic work achieved.

There was a concern amongst the senior officers in the Yard that if we did these things and the big dealers were arrested, they wanted to know where their credit was coming from in the work which we achieved. They always wanted their credit for the work. My men and I always found this very strange. We had no interest in any credentials or fame. We wanted to take bad things away from bad people who were being dangerous. All we wanted to do as front line troops was go out and arrest people, that was it. In those days, for some weird and strange reason, Customs believed that what you did was search people as they came through Dover, and then arrest people who had drugs on them, like the lorry driver. There was no further enquiry regarding where the drugs came from. Nobody was chasing the source of the drugs. But we were chasing them, and we wanted Customs to let the lorry run to its location, so we'd know what we needed to. We did good work and we could have done more great work if we were allowed to, if we were not used as collateral damage in Mark's Kelaher mission.

It's something that sticks in the mind after all these years but as I say, with all of it and despite the shattering of our lives and our wives' lives and those of our families and our friends, there really were some warm and funny days, great days, great memories: running around with radios that didn't work and being with no protection. Rarely did we have any weapons when the opposition did; we were offered bribes and threatened left and right. They were the best and the worst days of our lives. But when it was good, it was bloody great. There was no life balance, and it was completely consuming, but it was an honour dealing with low life street creepers and highly cunning dangerous men. It took over my life but like I said, fact is stranger than fiction; maybe that's why the whole thing felt like being on the telly! Yep, it really was a classic era. I used to get home some nights past midnight, fall into bed completely knackered and the phone would go. I'd be getting dressed again within the hour, and getting back to the office. But I loved it, working with a straight team who were totally sound. I will never forget them.

If I was the Walrus, I guess that would be fair. Walruses are relatively long-lived, social animals, and they are considered to be a 'keystone species' who have a big effect despite being of a small number. The adult walrus is easily recognized by its tusks, whiskers, and bulk. They are also hunted for their meat, fat, skin, tusks, and bone. If I was the Walrus, so were all the good men I worked with bound by an oath of honesty, and a shared desire to kick-start this country's war on drugs. Despite how we were hunted for our skins, we live on.

I am Norman Pilcher. I do not know if John Lennon was talking about me but I say to you all... *I Am The Walrus!*

And that was my final police report.

I leave you now, bid you farewell and suggest you behave. That's right: 'Once a copper, always a copper.'

Appendix

Some notes on just one of the many examples of misinformation over the years!

No matter what line of work one follows, there should be a definite sense of inner satisfaction in what one chooses as a career path. I found this to be true with my work but it is important if you find this, not to expect everyone to consider the work you do as having any worth. You will always find those who disapprove of the results you obtain and the work achieved. In the line of duty, it is obvious that we were going to make enemies with those we dealt with and also with their supporters. This was made plain in stories that were the subject of publication. Examples of this are shown in the book *Butterfly On A Wheel: The Great Rolling Stones Drugs Bust*, written by Simon Wells. As I've never been given the opportunity to respond to Wells and his writings; I refer to the 2011 publication of the book here:

Pages 65–68: To say that our unit dressed with a hint of 'gangster' is ridiculous, in fact laughable, and written only to glamorise. We dressed in a casual manner. The section stating that we dealt with a singer known as Donovan and the recollections of a man known as 'Gypsy' Dave Mills is also not true. At no time did I ever apply for a search warrant relating to any address occupied by a person named Donovan even if that person may have thought that I did. The language used in these writings is brightly coloured and designed to entice with lurid detail but neither I nor any members of our unit have ever had any contact with any person mentioned in these pages. Due to such writings, I became a folklore bogeyman to a collective youth who needed and desired an enemy of the times. I came to learn that celebrities enjoyed saying that they were 'busted by the Drugs Squad' and that the Drugs Squad was... me, to be perfectly blunt. But they were doing this for their own status as many of them wished and desired to be as admired as

John Lennon was and they thought that one way to obtain this admiration in the public domain was to claim I arrested them. I happen to know that it was a team from Sussex that went up and arrested the person called Donovan, so in fact it was actually nothing to do with the Met.

Page 139: There is mention here of a hookah pipe seized at Heathrow airport which was displayed on my desk – totally untrue.

Page 146: We did arrest Brian separately to this alleged search but here, there is a description of a search carried out by our unit that did not happen. This supposed search was in Courtfield Road, apparently led by myself, and it is suggested that because of my so-called questionable reputation the drugs found had been 'planted' at the premises.

Page 223: There was never any 'covert surveillance' in relation to the members of the Rolling Stones by our unit.

Page 229: As previously outlined, Donovan was never known to our unit.

Page 251: I never visited Jones at 17 Chesham Street in relation to a murder enquiry which was noted in police records – such an event never happened.

Page 257: Reference is made to comments made by Caroline Coon, for whom I had a high regard, which claimed that people were arrested and then that they went missing for several weeks (the implication was that police were responsible for them allegedly going missing). Any person arrested would be charged and then duly appear before a court. Caroline also alleged that police would search a property, steal money, assault persons, and plant drugs and generally abuse them. Nothing could be further from the truth in relation to cases dealt with by our unit.

Pages 273–276: No search was carried out at Chesham Street as stated; in fact no search warrant was ever applied for by our unit. There was no attempt to search premises at Kenwood allegedly occupied by John Lennon in 1968. This account by 'Donovan' and 'Gypsy' Dave Mills is without foundation.

In the same year it is claimed that we were interested in the activities of Eric

Clapton and that we were keeping observation on his address at 152 Kings Road, Chelsea. It is further claimed that Clapton had been warned that we were intending to raid his address, this being passed on by Caroline Coon as the result of information received from local police. I had never worked at Chelsea police station. Our unit never at any time carried out a search of the property occupied by Clapton. The reference to Detective Sergeant Robin Constable is not valid as he was never on the staff at the Drugs Squad and most certainly not a colleague of mine.

From this, readers can now more easily understand how these falsities perpetuate the folklore surrounding my name and our unit. To date, if you read the Wikipedia page of Norman Pilcher, it is written, largely I would imagine due to a continuation of these original writings, that: 'Eric Clapton was nearly arrested at The Pheasantry on drugs charges, but escaped from the rear of the building when Pilcher rang the doorbell to announce "Postman, special delivery".' Again, our unit did not carry out a search of the property occupied by Eric Clapton. It is my belief that as soon as these stories are seeded into the public discourse, they root, spread and grow new heads. It has been shocking to read the creative stories over the years since I retired. I did have information about Eric Clapton but I never went to The Pheasantry. I never had any serious intent on him because the information had been given to me by a chap who had said he was a friend of his. I came to the conclusion that he was trying to work off some kind of vendetta so I ignored it. There was so much baloney like this at the time, I became used to it quite quickly.

Pages 283–286: It is true to say that a raid was carried out on the premises occupied by Tubby Hayes. As a result he was arrested but it was clear to me that Tubby required medical assistance, urgently. With the help of his close friend we arranged for Tubby to be treated at Charing Cross Hospital. I took a keen interest in his care, but despite our efforts he later died of heart problems, which was very sad, as he was such a fabulous musician.

As to the raid on John Lennon's address, this has been well documented. At no time were any plea bargains discussed with Lennon, the master being dealt with by his legal team. As to the question put down in Parliament by Arthur Lewis MP: this was fully answered even to the point made by Mr Lewis that police should inform suspects to expect a raid.

As to the raid at George Harrison's address, which was allegedly arranged to coincide with the wedding of Paul McCartney: this is again fiction as there had been no publicity regarding the wedding, of which we were unaware. This search was carried out after the arrival home of Harrison in the presence of his lawyer. There was no clamouring around and the search and subsequent actions were carried out in a respectful manner. After discussing the overall situation regarding drug use with Harrison, my opinion was hardened against the position that possession users should be given criminal records.

Pages 294–295: At no time did any member of the Drugs Squad 'plant' drugs on any suspect during raids. It is quite obvious that any such action would have put our careers in jeopardy. There has never been any evidence to support such an allegation apart from remarks made by those who wished to cause us problems. There are other examples published around our work, which are based on non-truths being passed to the authors, which they deemed to be suitable for publication.

Lightning Source UK Ltd.
Milton Keynes UK
UKHW012214141120
373401UK00001B/101